The Four Seasons through Photographs

by Jane Ballard
Jane Ballard Photography

As a photographer who rarely has the opportunity to travel far from home, I focus on the world around me. Using my Nikon digital camera, I enjoy capturing local icons and scenery. Most of my photographs are realistic representations, where I use editing programs mostly for color enhancement, sharpening, and cropping. My favorite photographs are printed on metal or metallic paper, but, one way or another, they MUST be printed to be enjoyed properly!

I am venturing more into the abstract, photographing ordinary things and presenting them in a new way. I use oil and water, fire, fairy lights, blacklights, among other things to create images that are barely recognizable as the commodities that they really are!

I regard my photographs as specific captures of time never to be reproduced exactly as they were the first time I recorded them. I enjoy sharing my perspective with all who wish to see!

I hope YOU enjoy my images, too! This is my first venture into a printed magazine-style presentation of my captures and I hope it's the first of many themed photo books to come!

I DO have plans (and plenty of images) for more!

Jane Ballard

PS - A really big THANK YOU goes to my husband, Bobby, who entertains me nearly every weekend with travels throughout the Four State area searching for that "perfect shot"!

Winter is an etching, Spring a watercolor, Summer an oil painting, and Autumn a mosaic of them all.   Stanley Horowitz

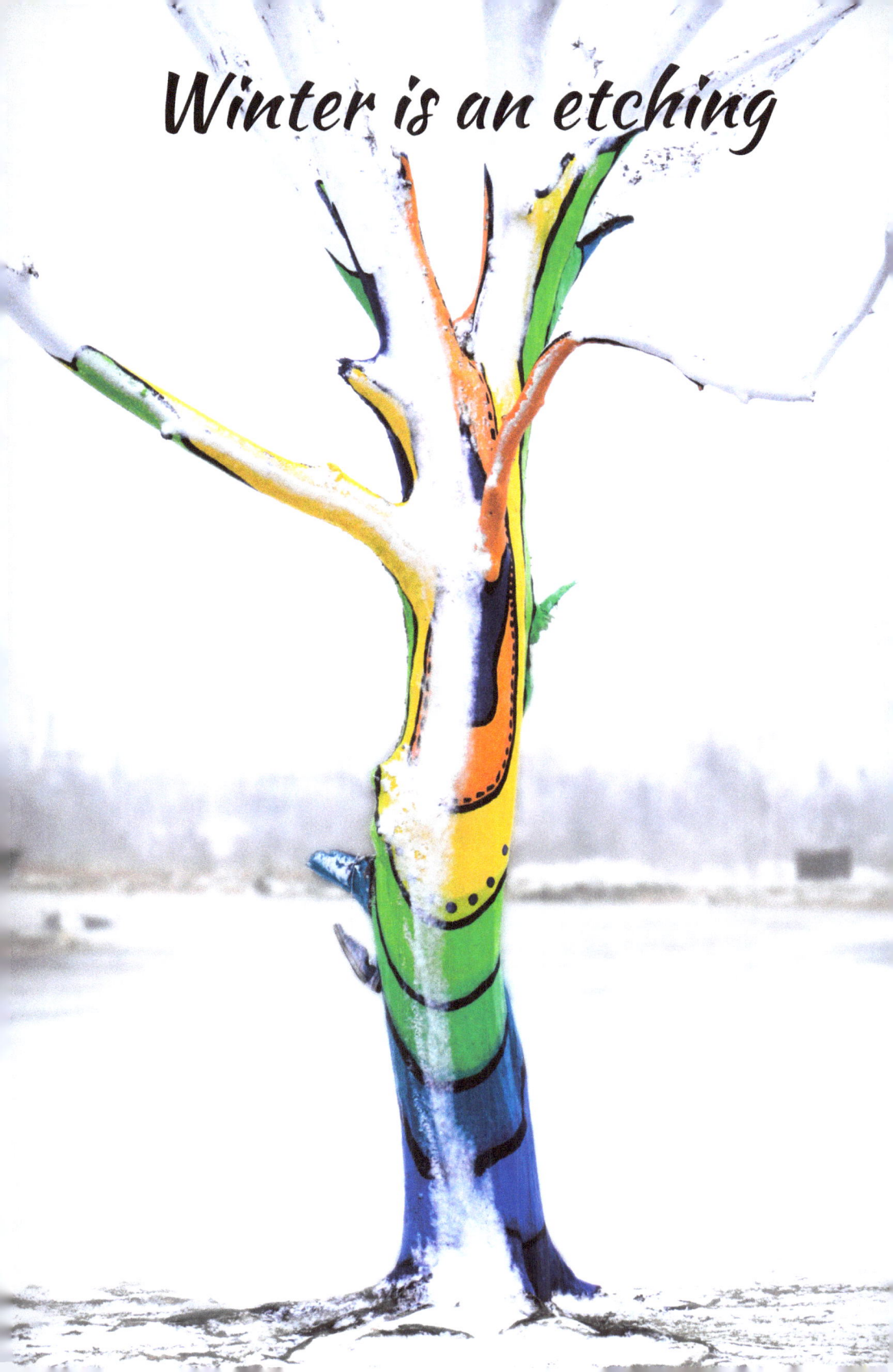

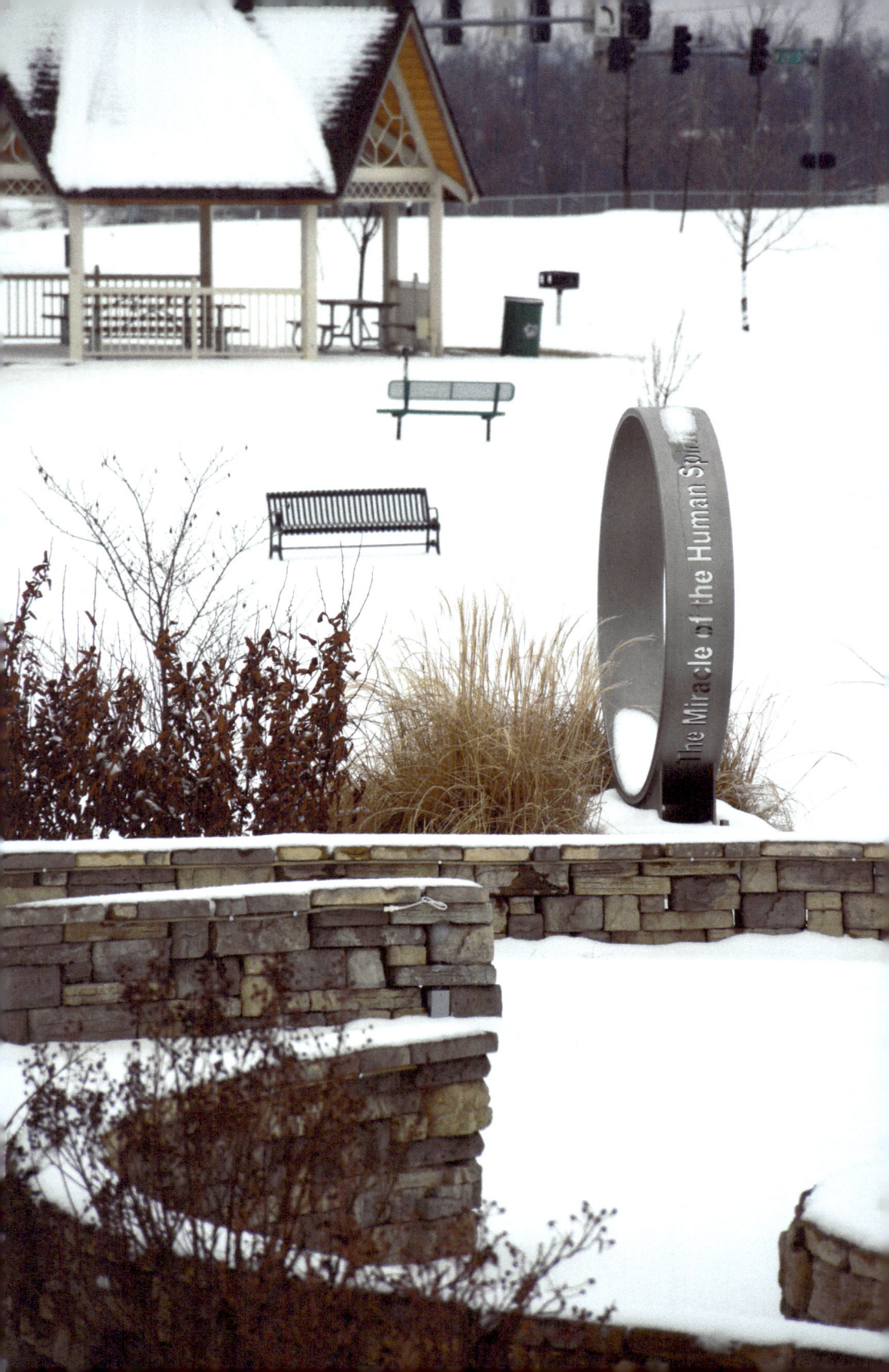

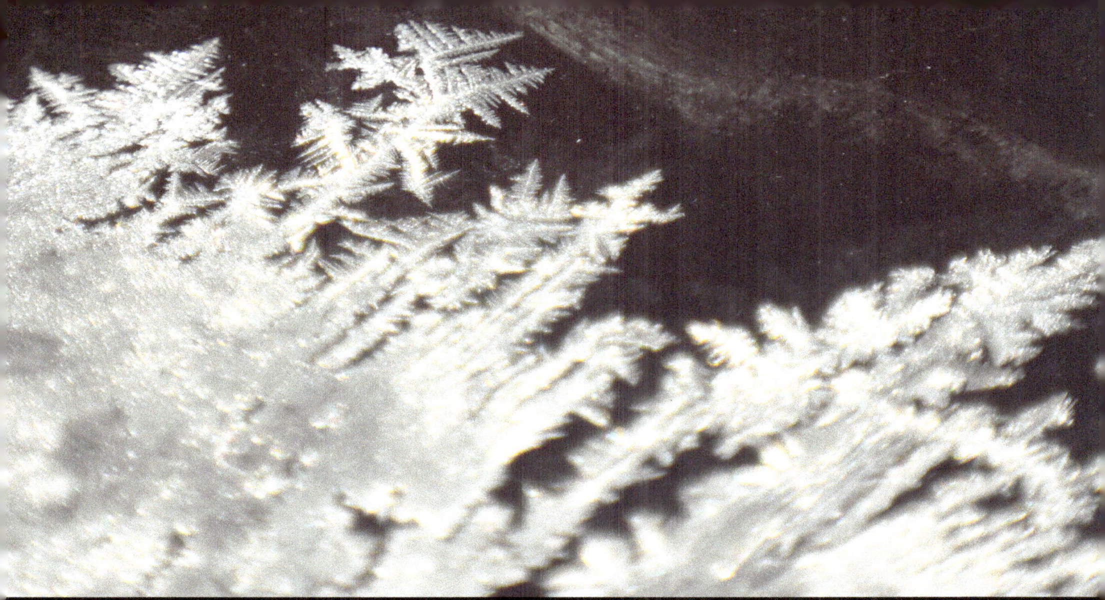

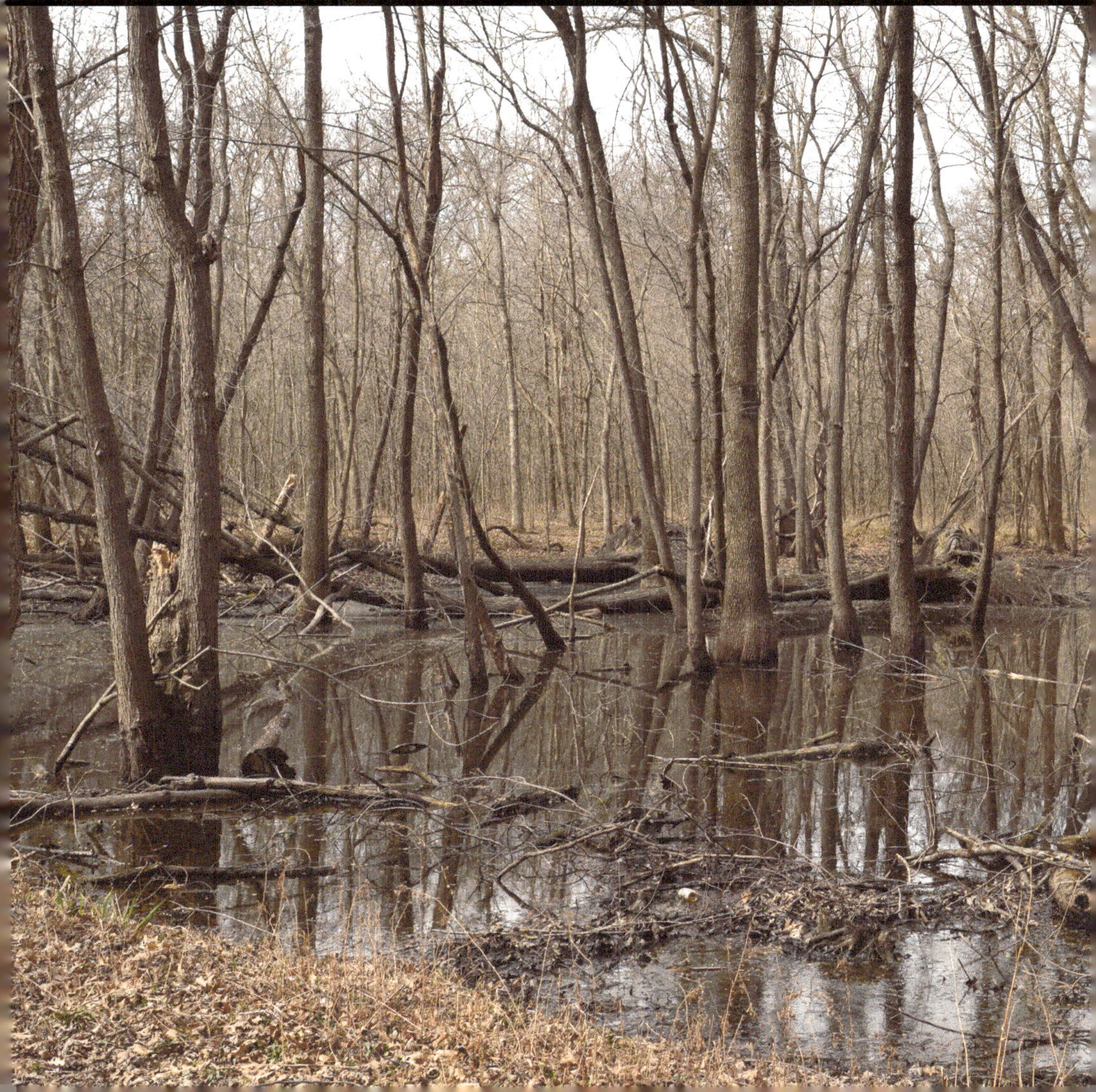

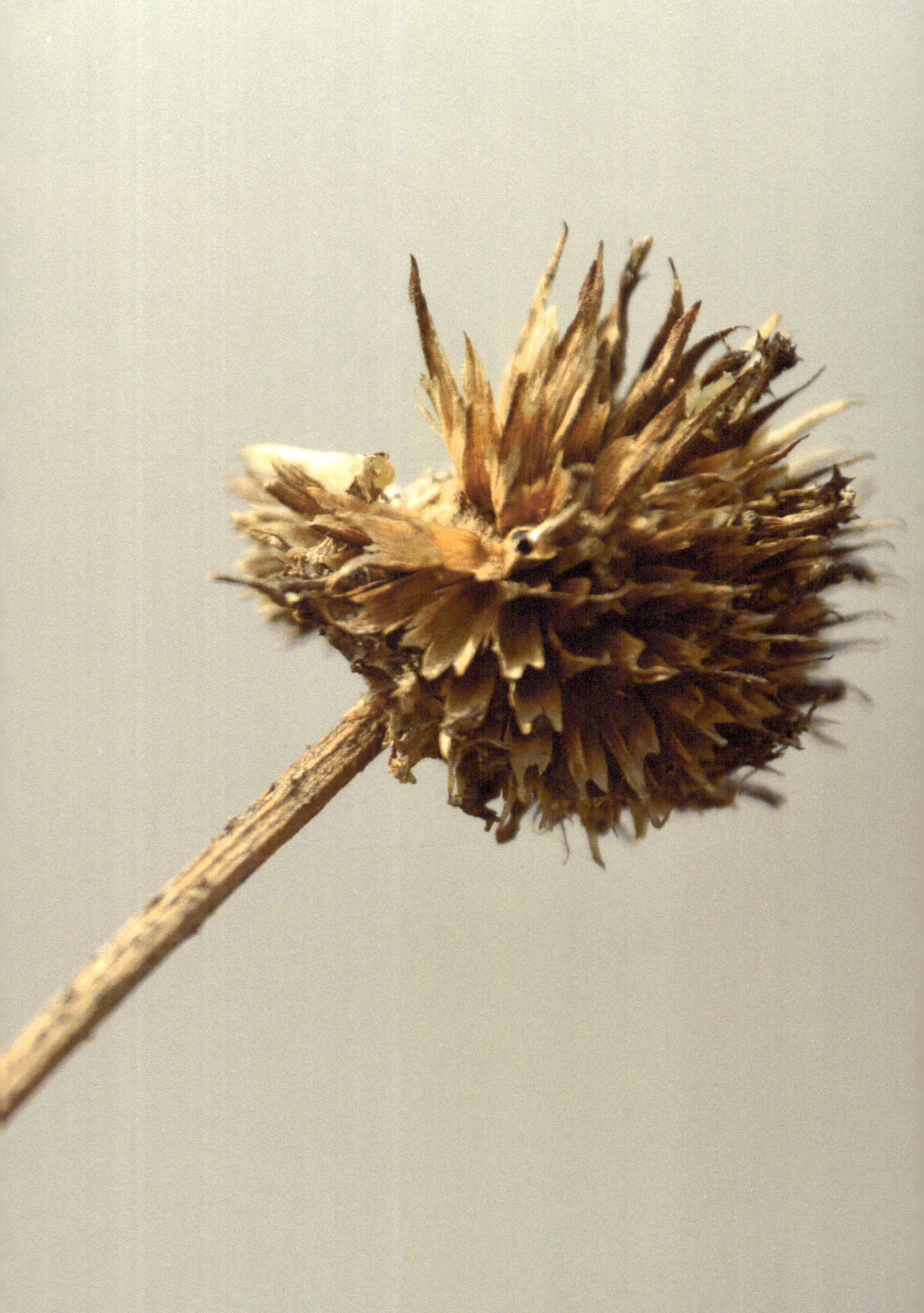

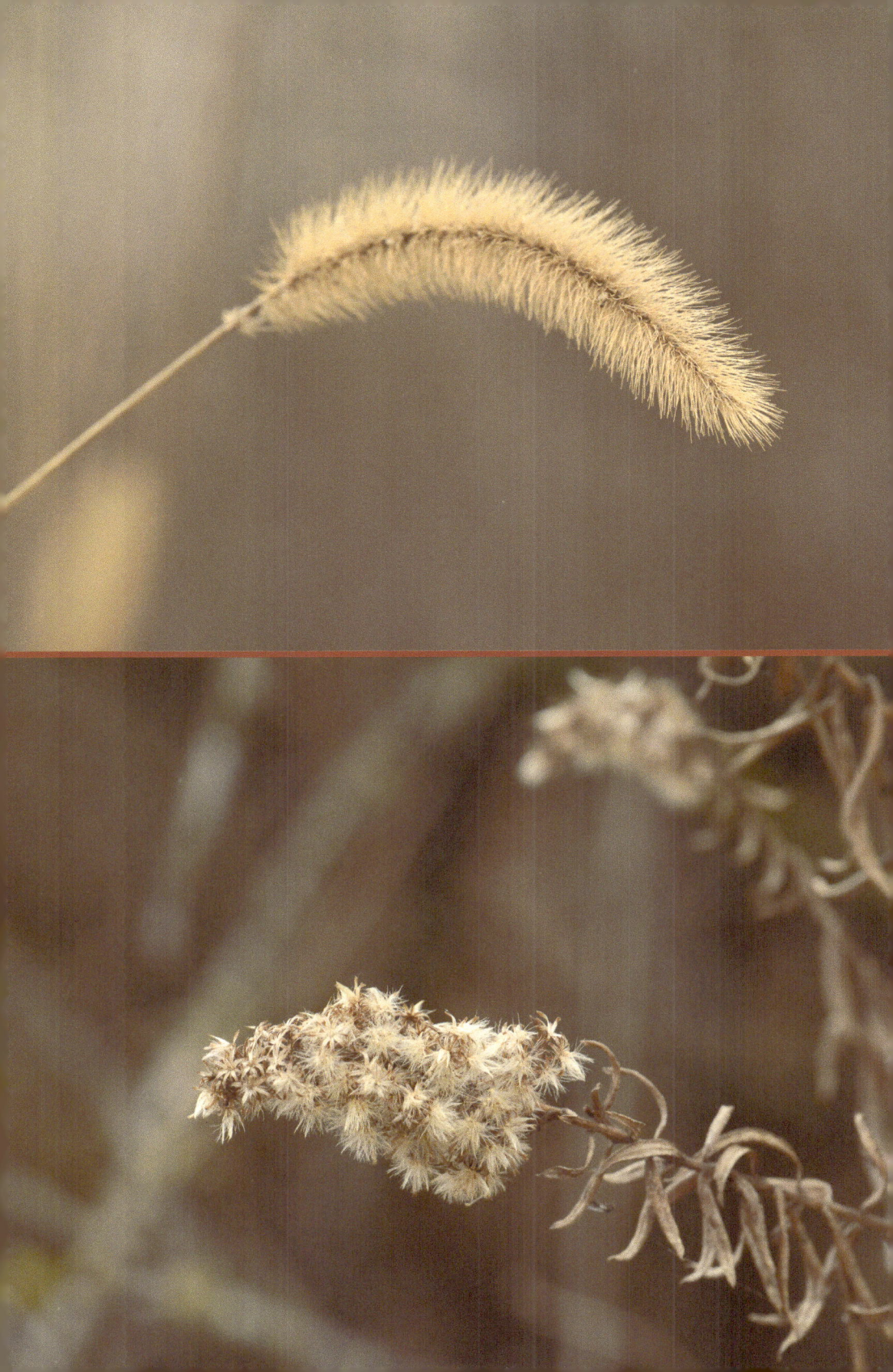

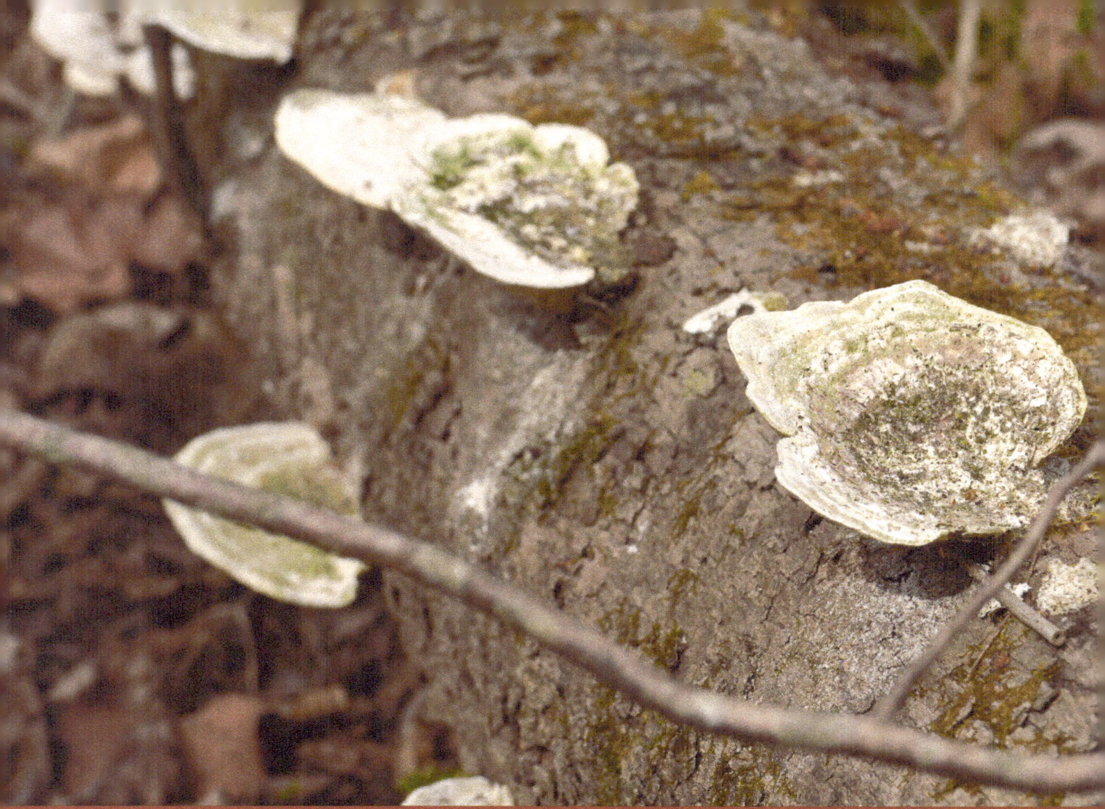

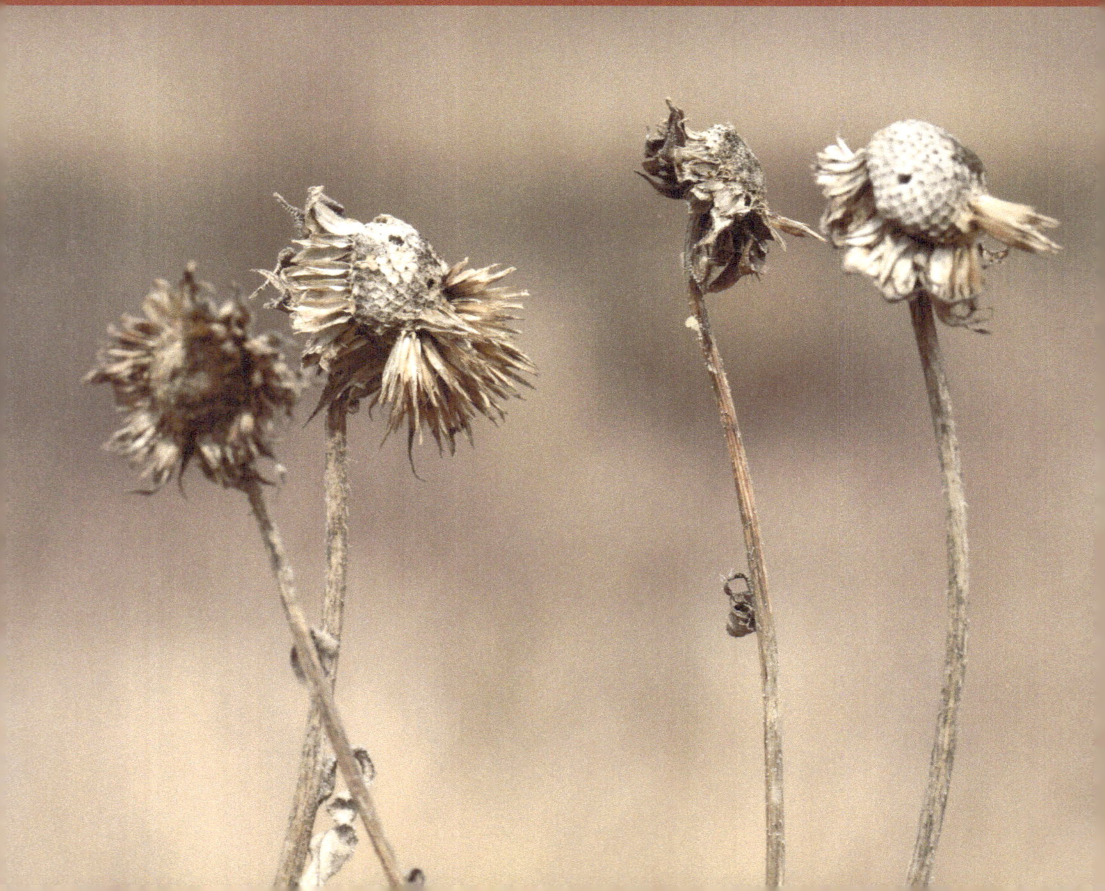

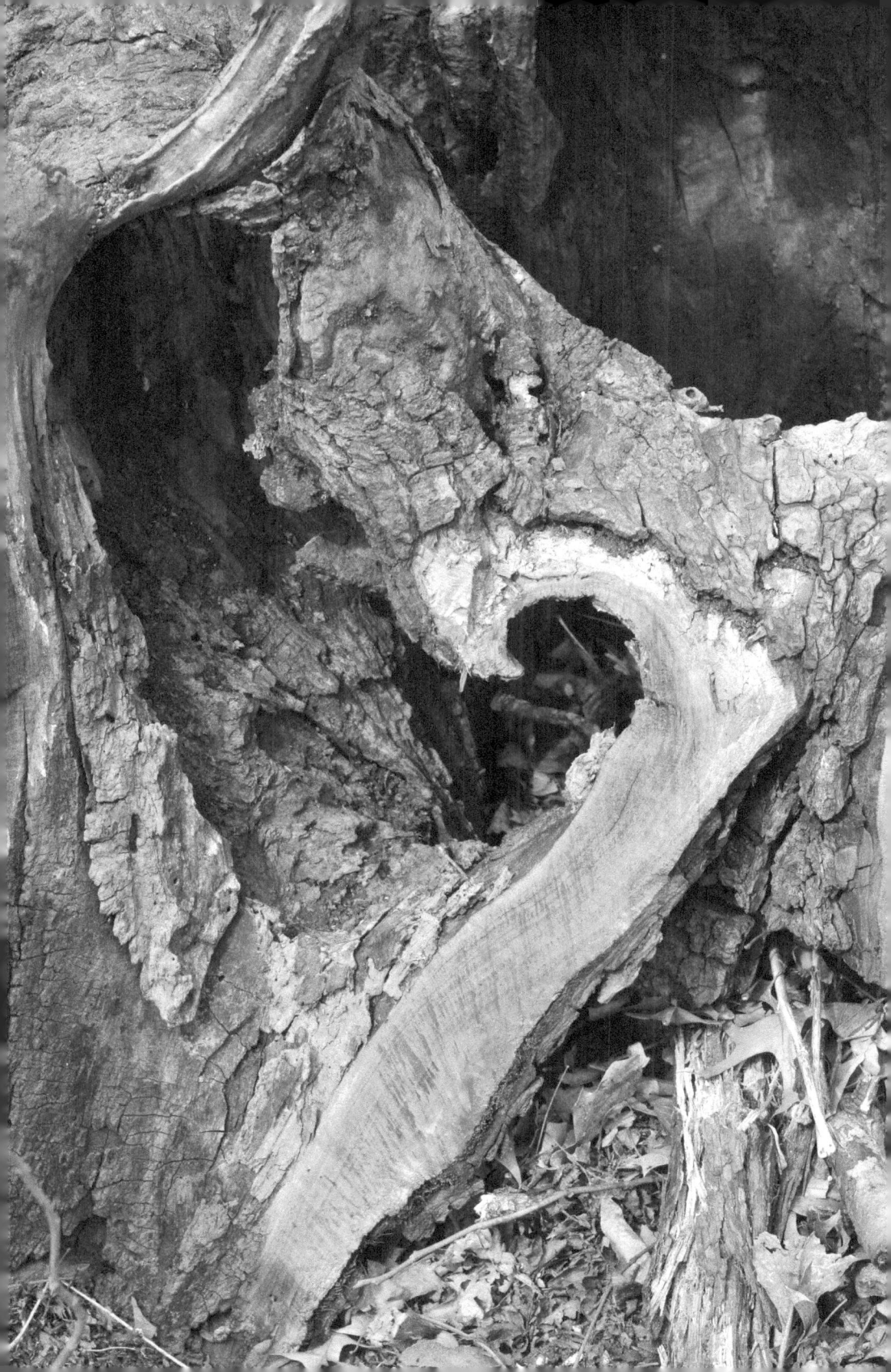

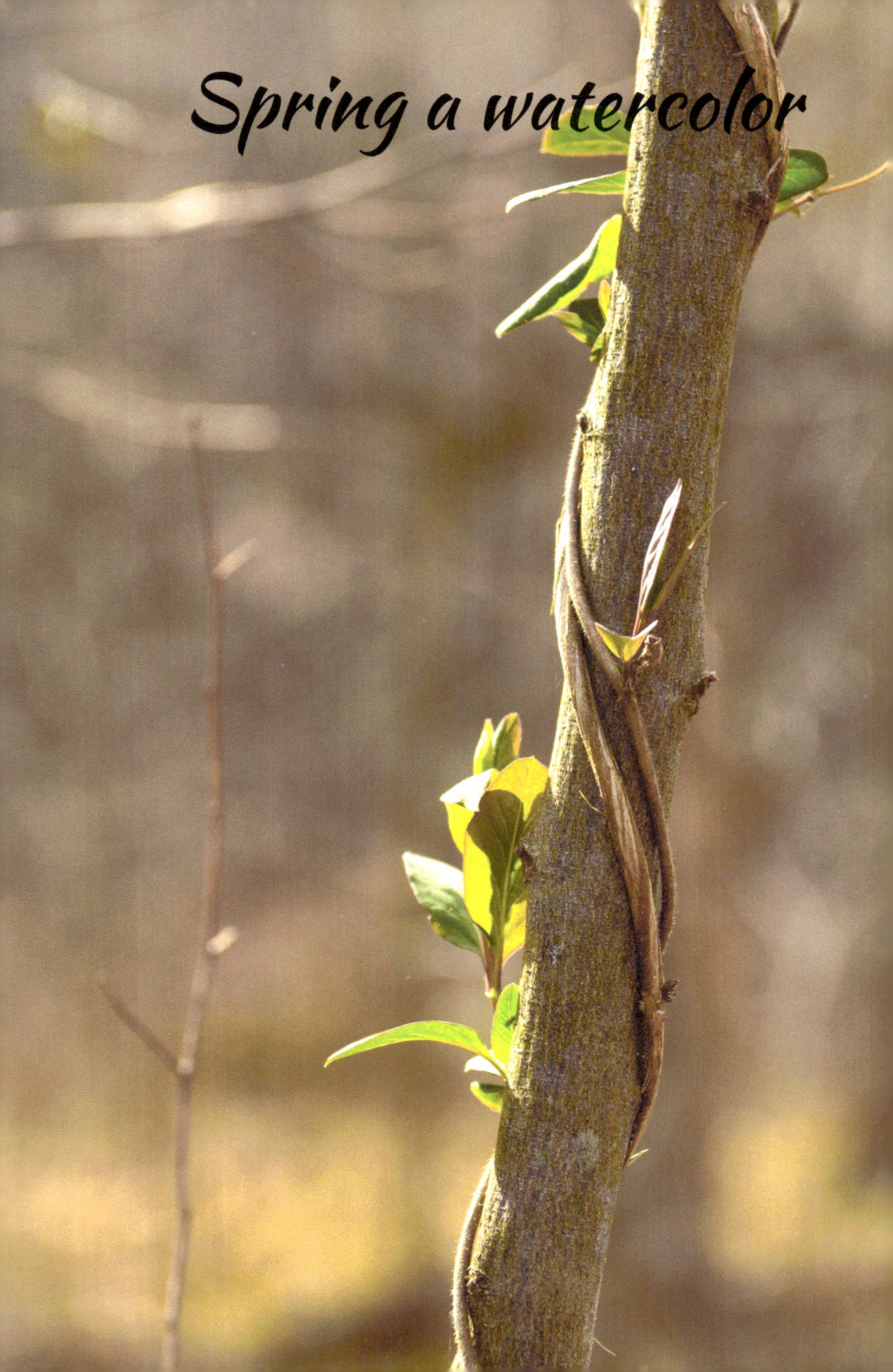

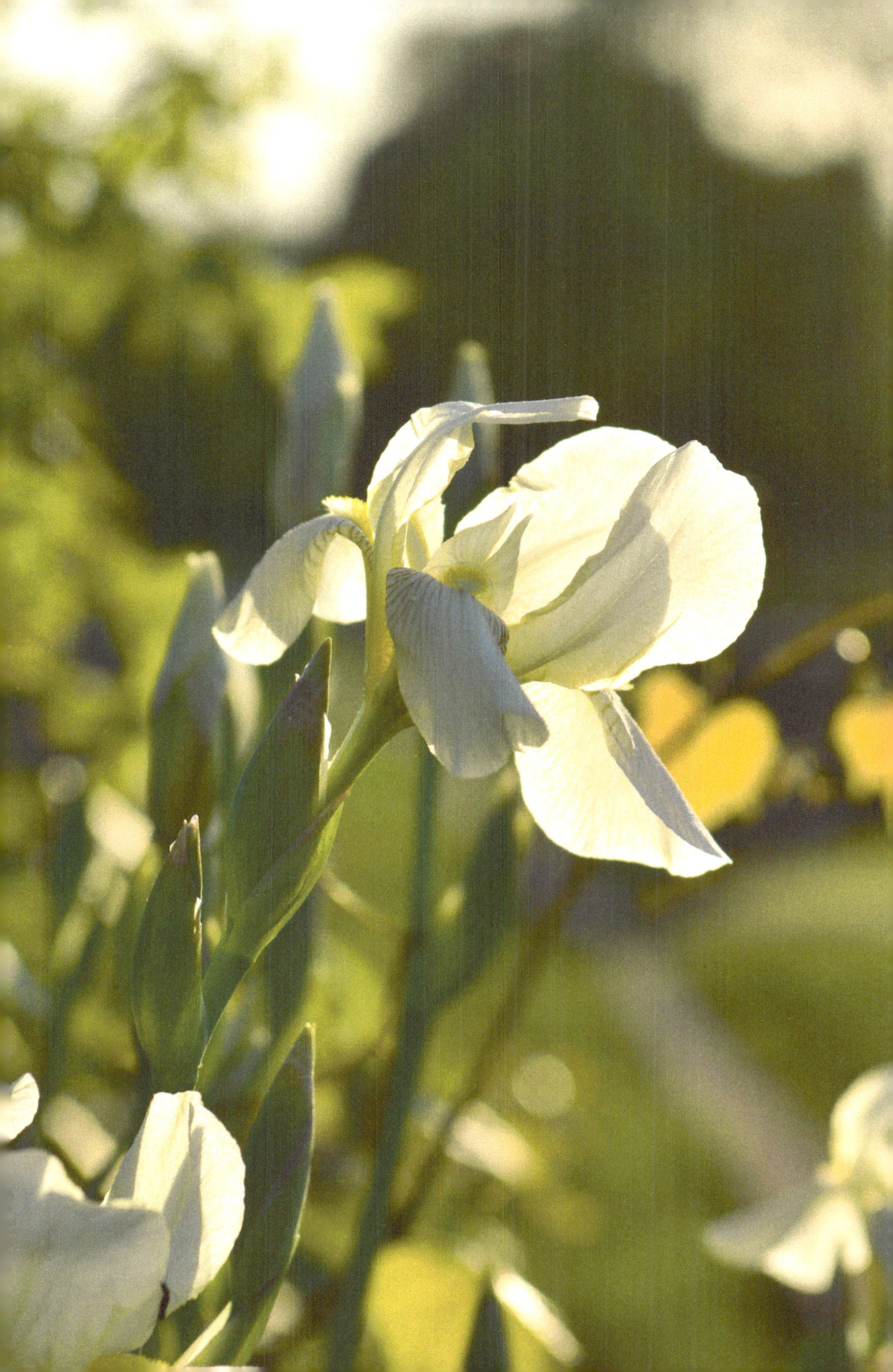

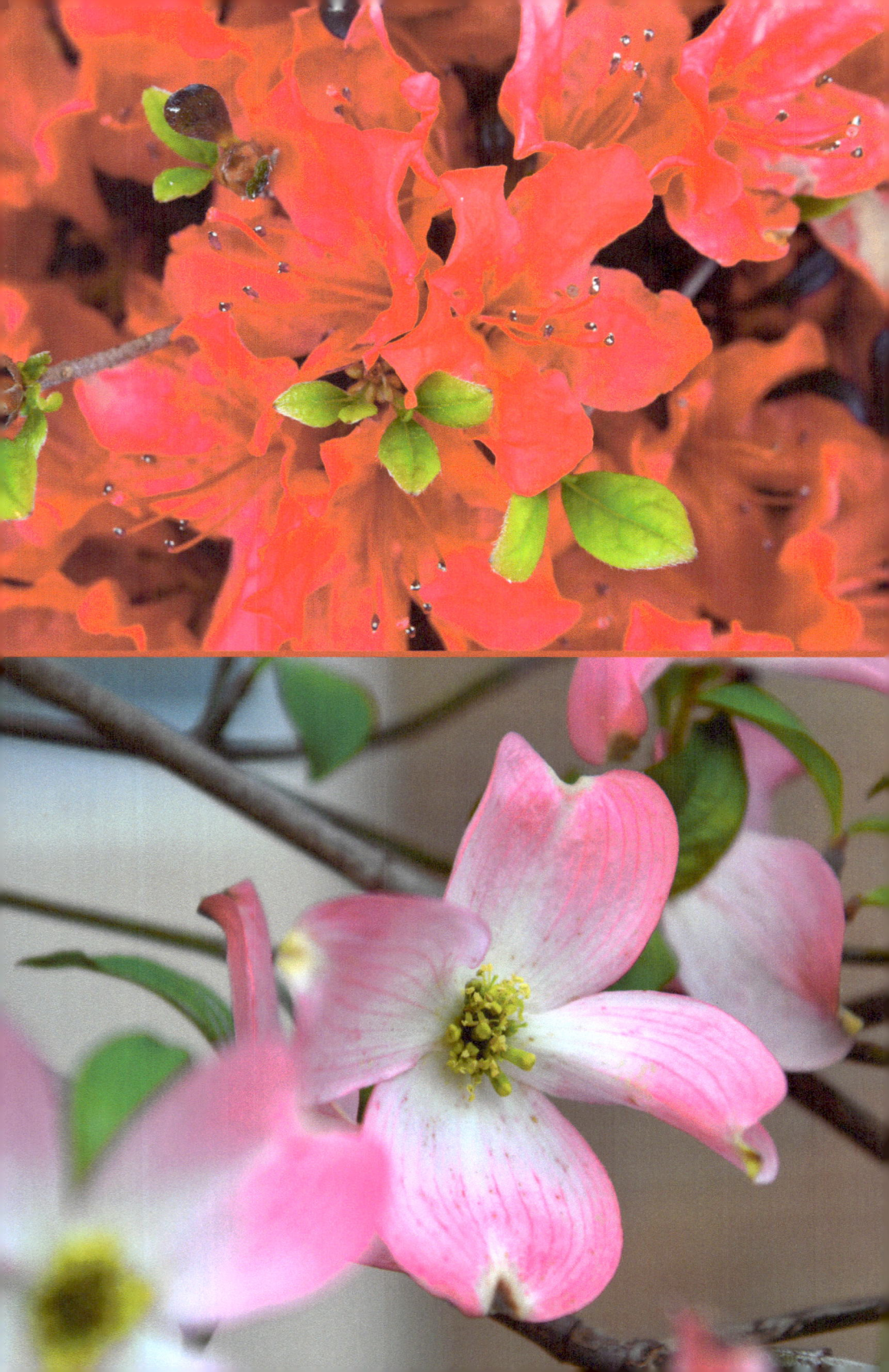

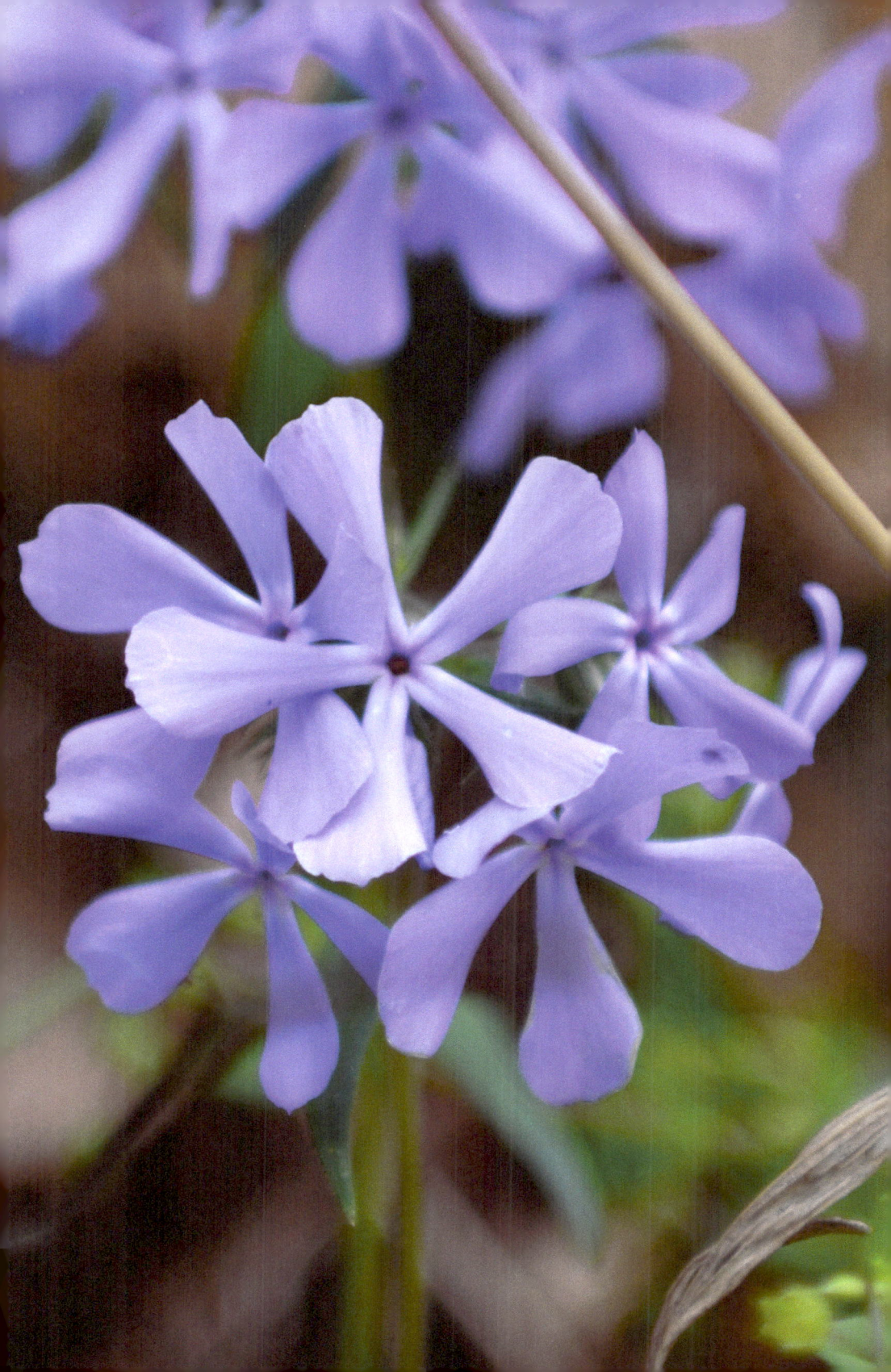

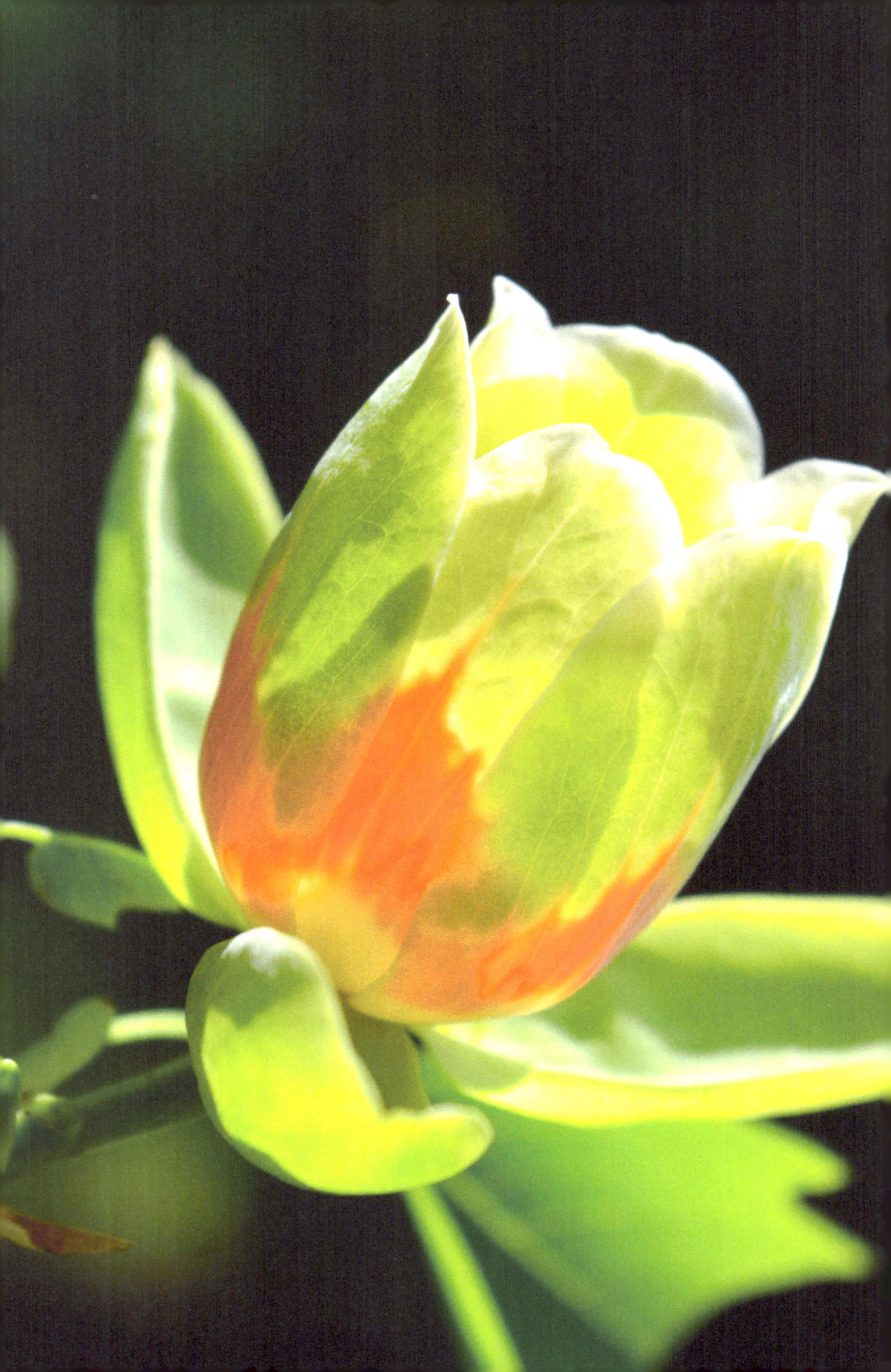

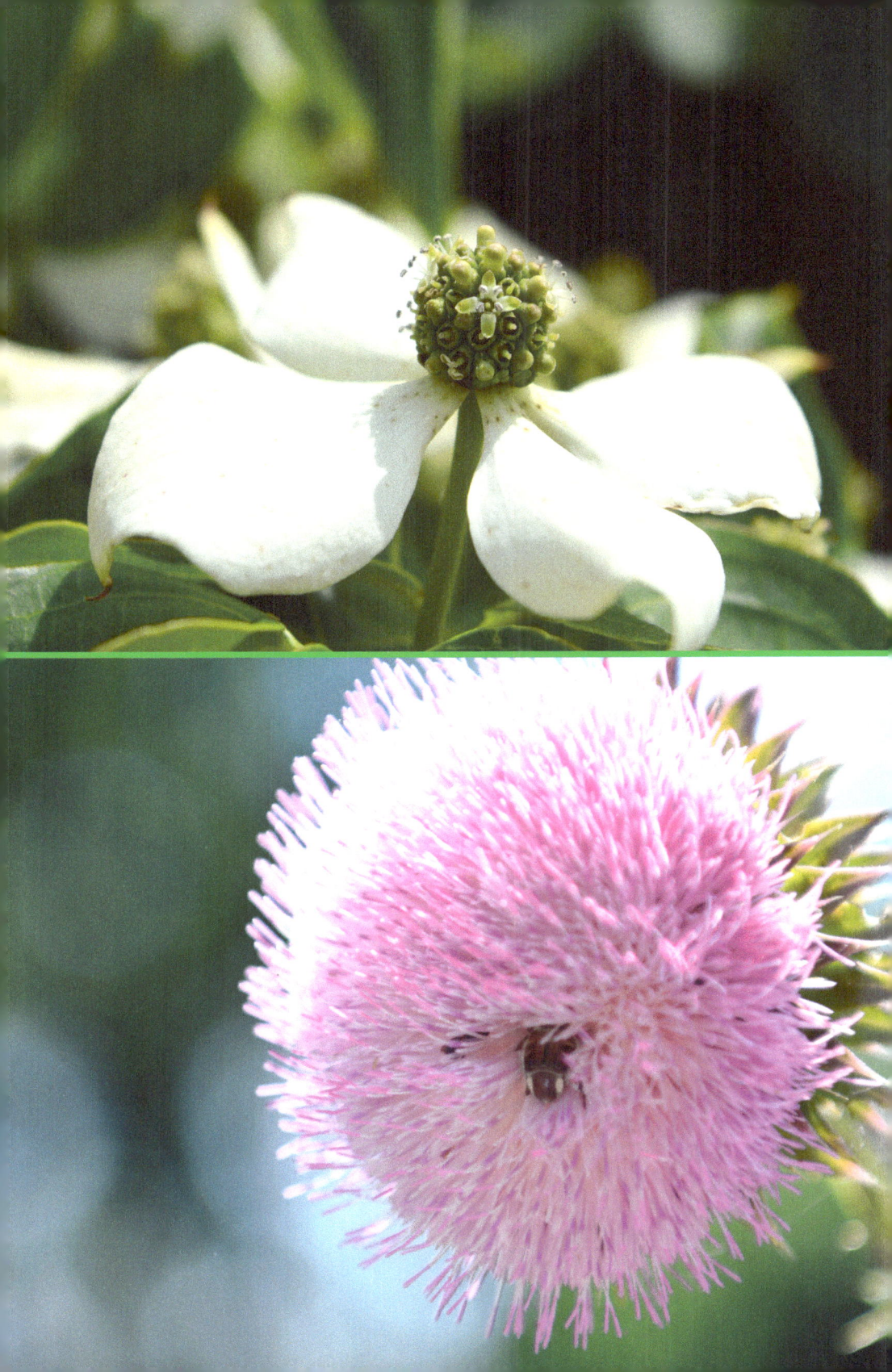

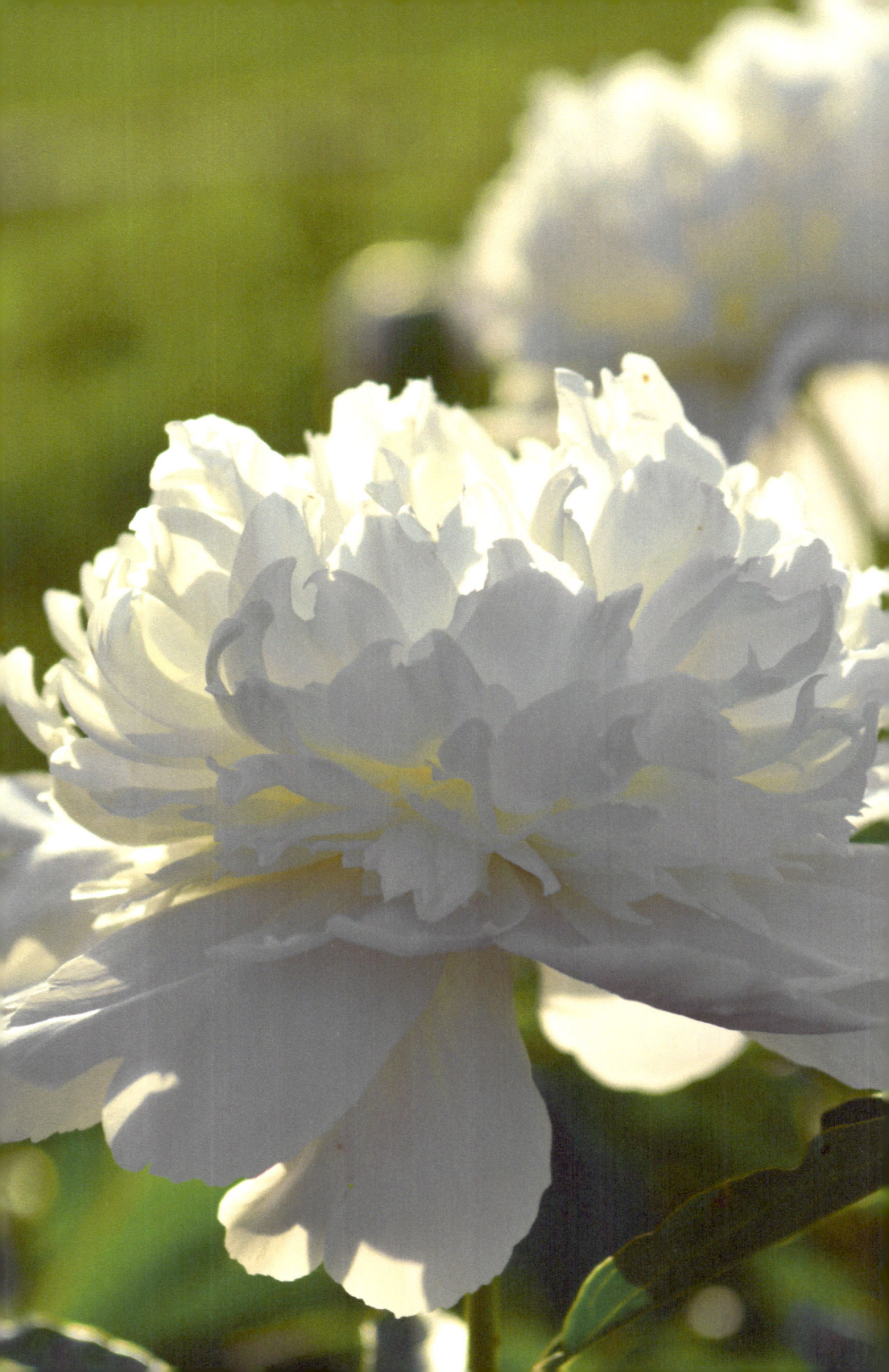

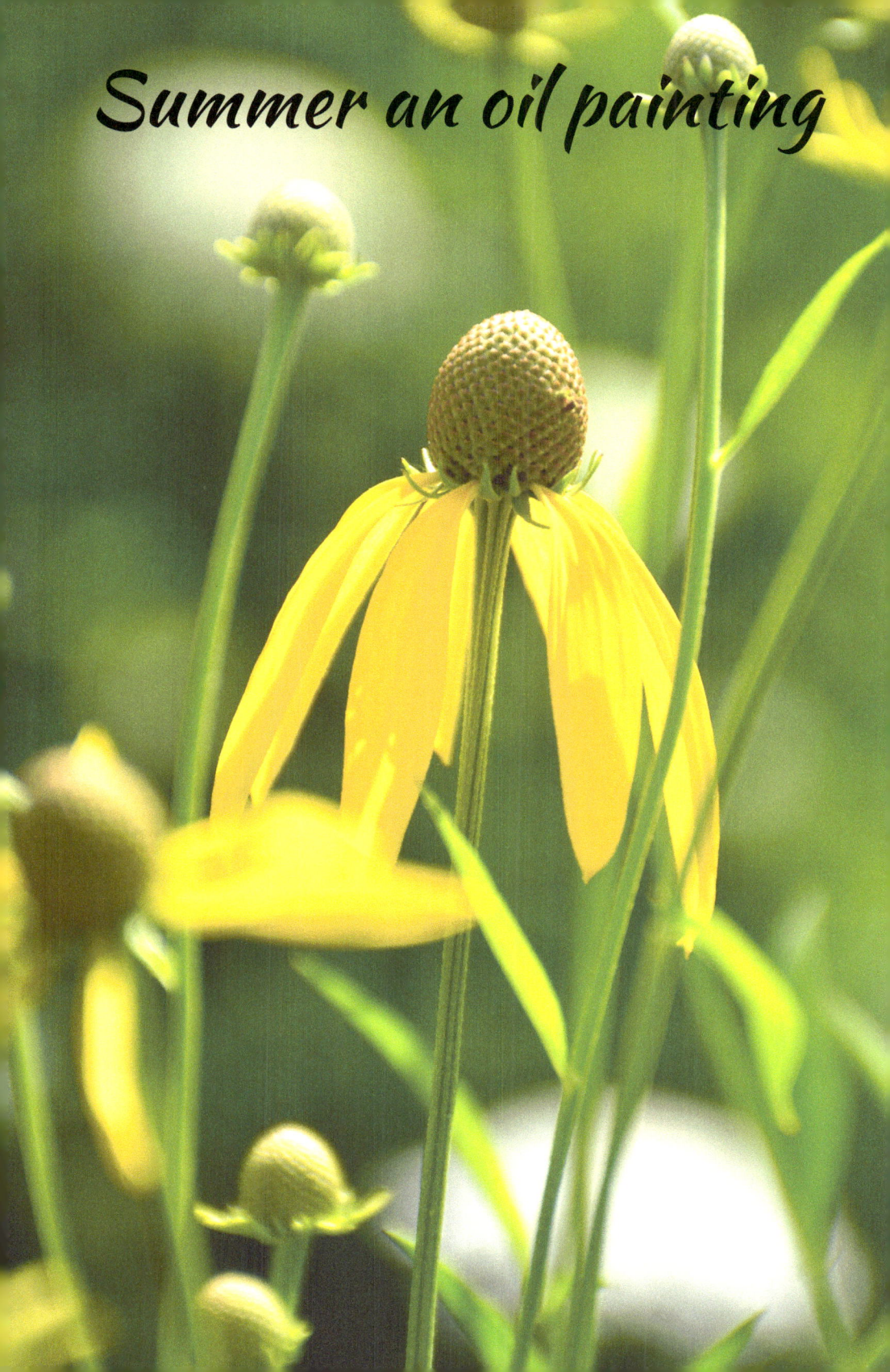
Summer an oil painting

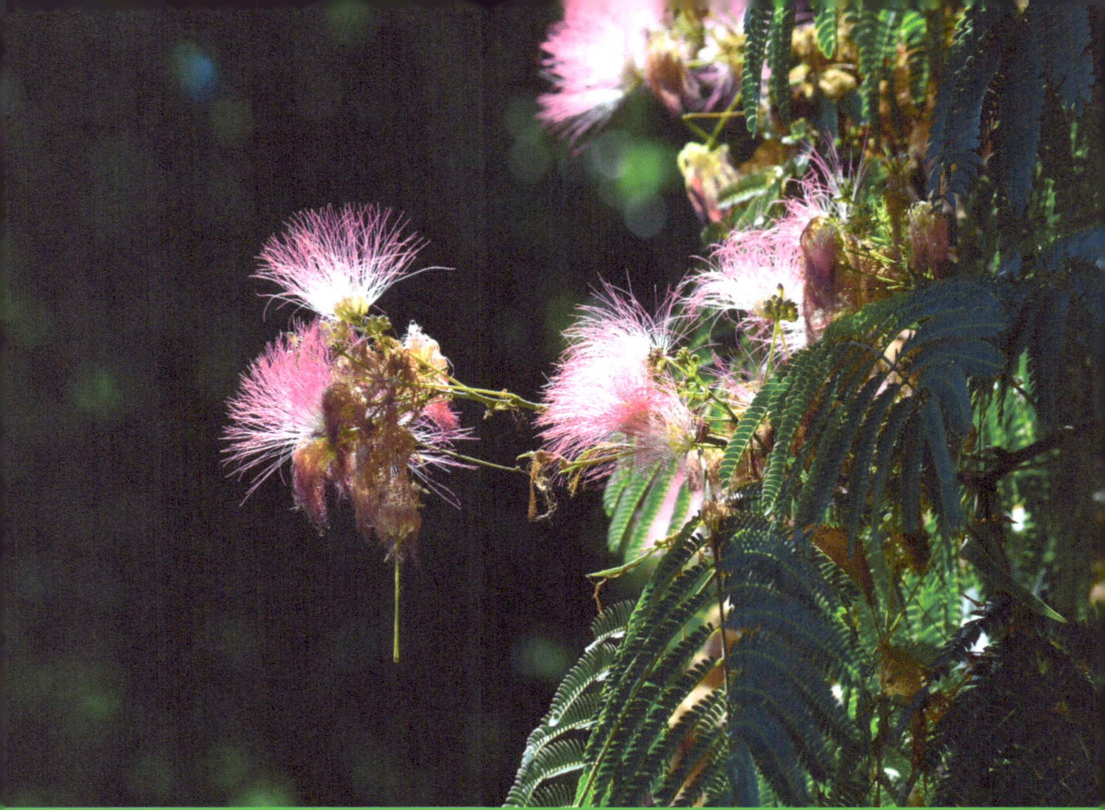

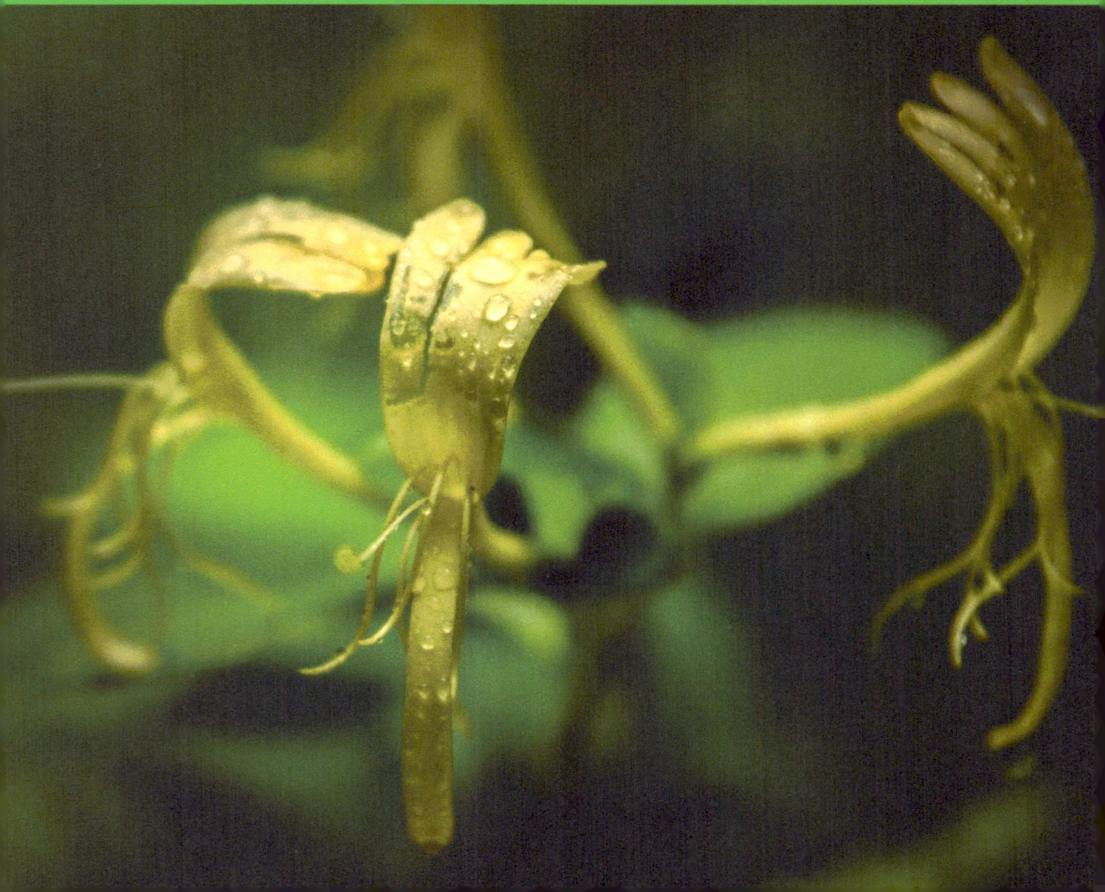

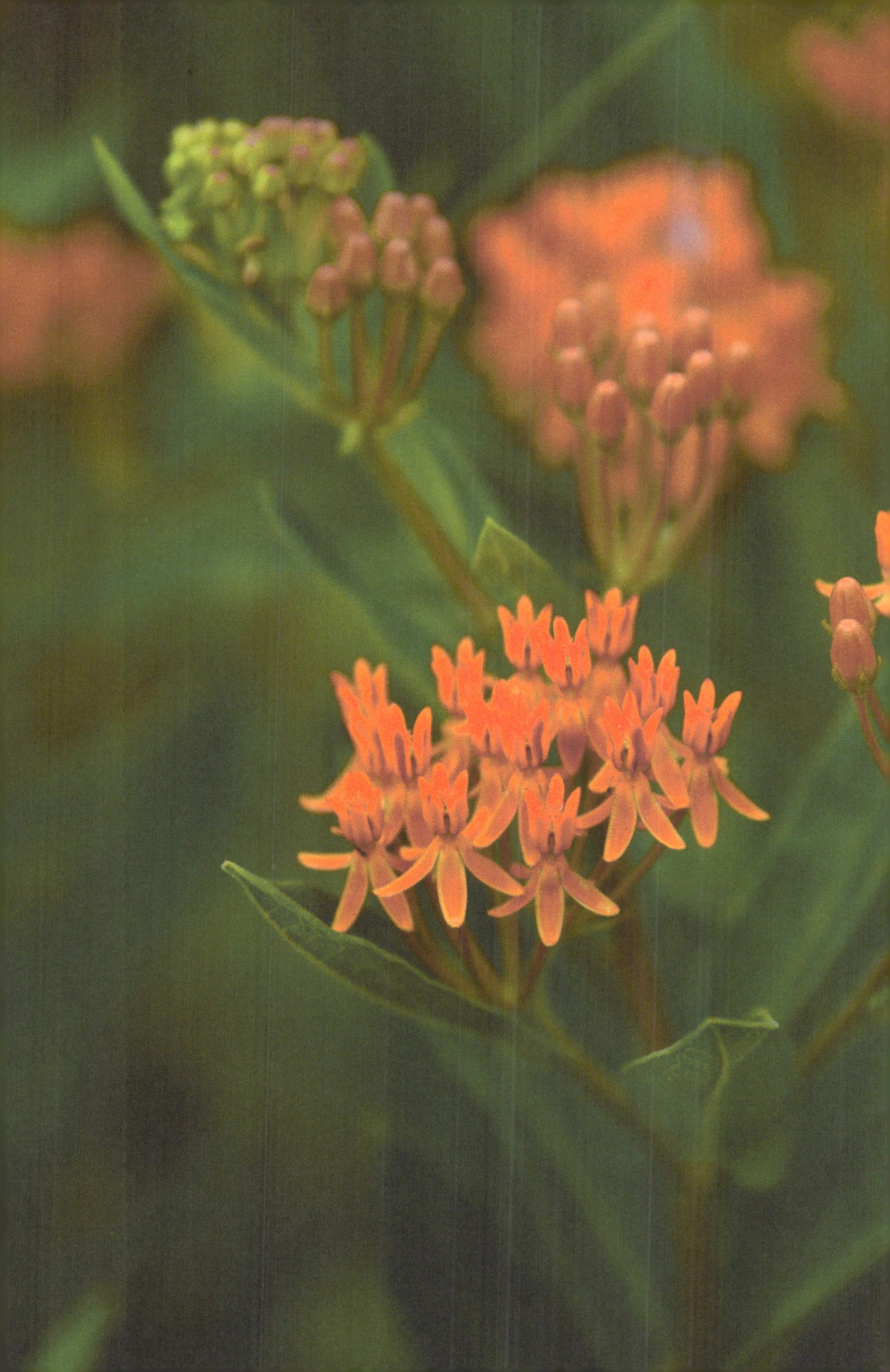

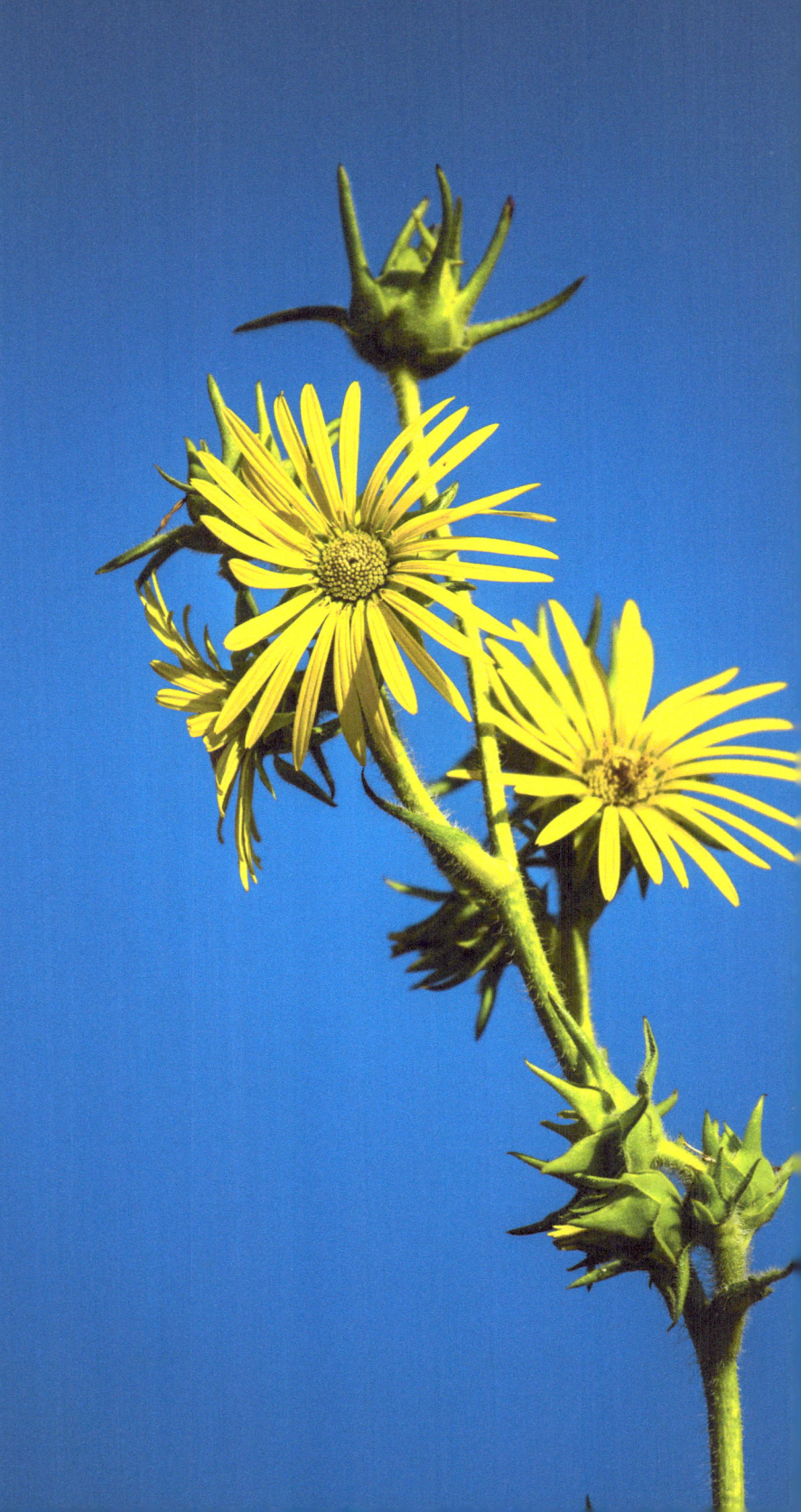

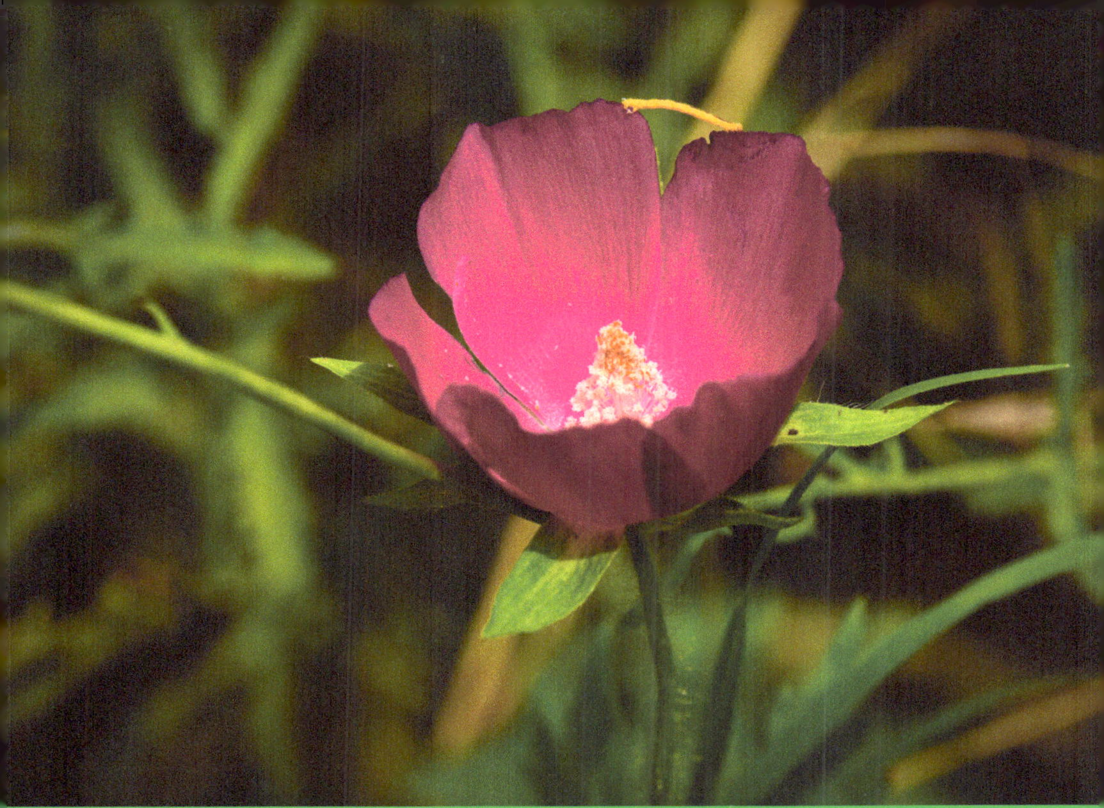

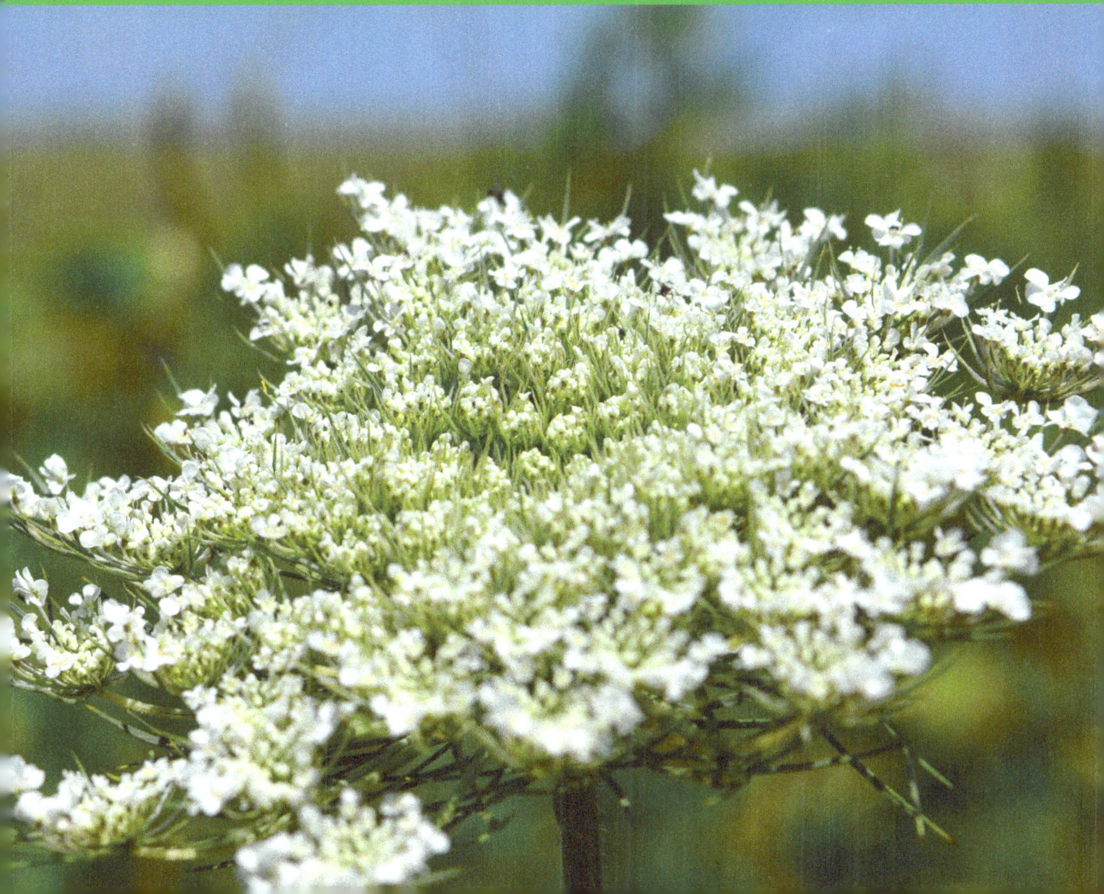

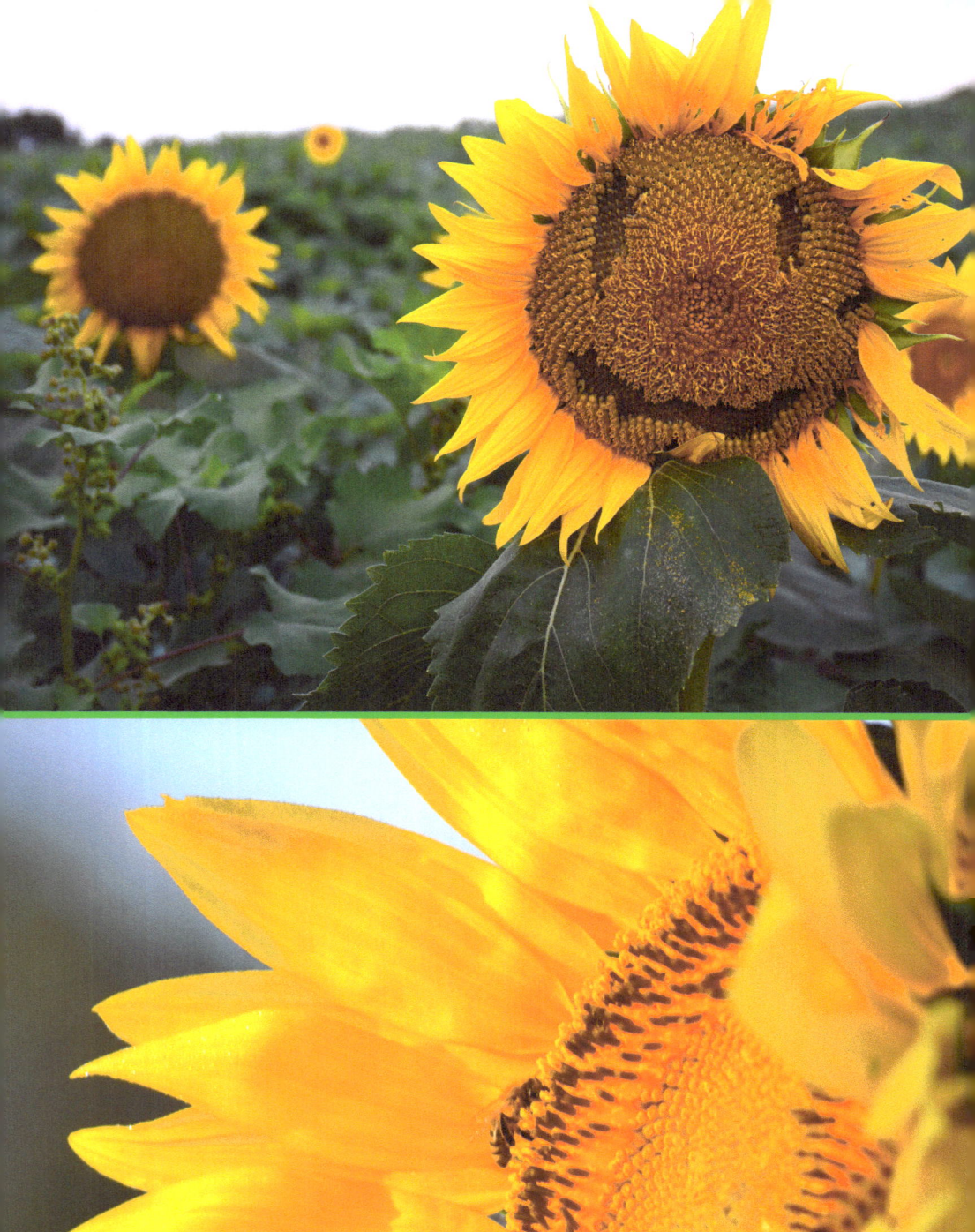

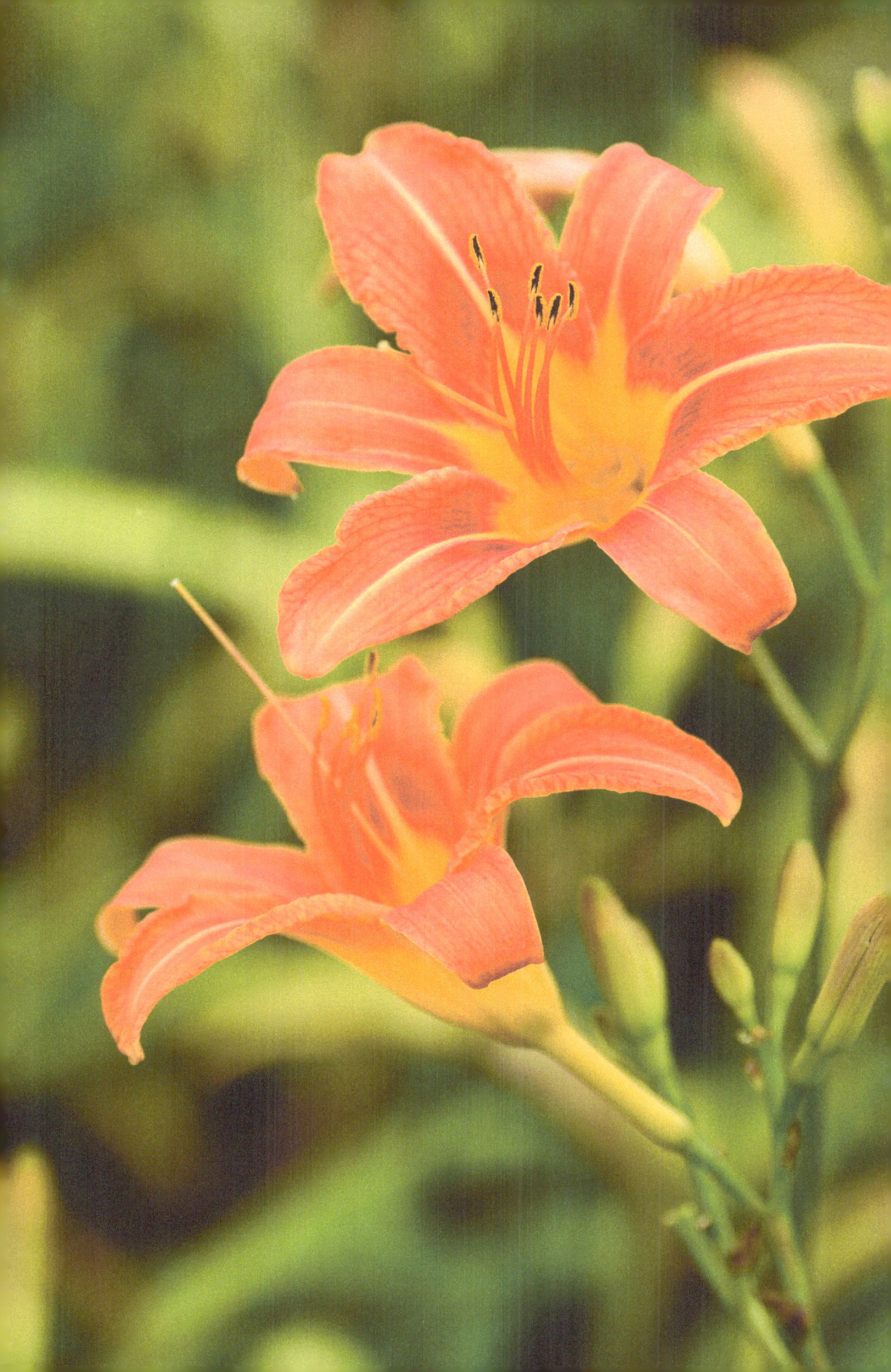

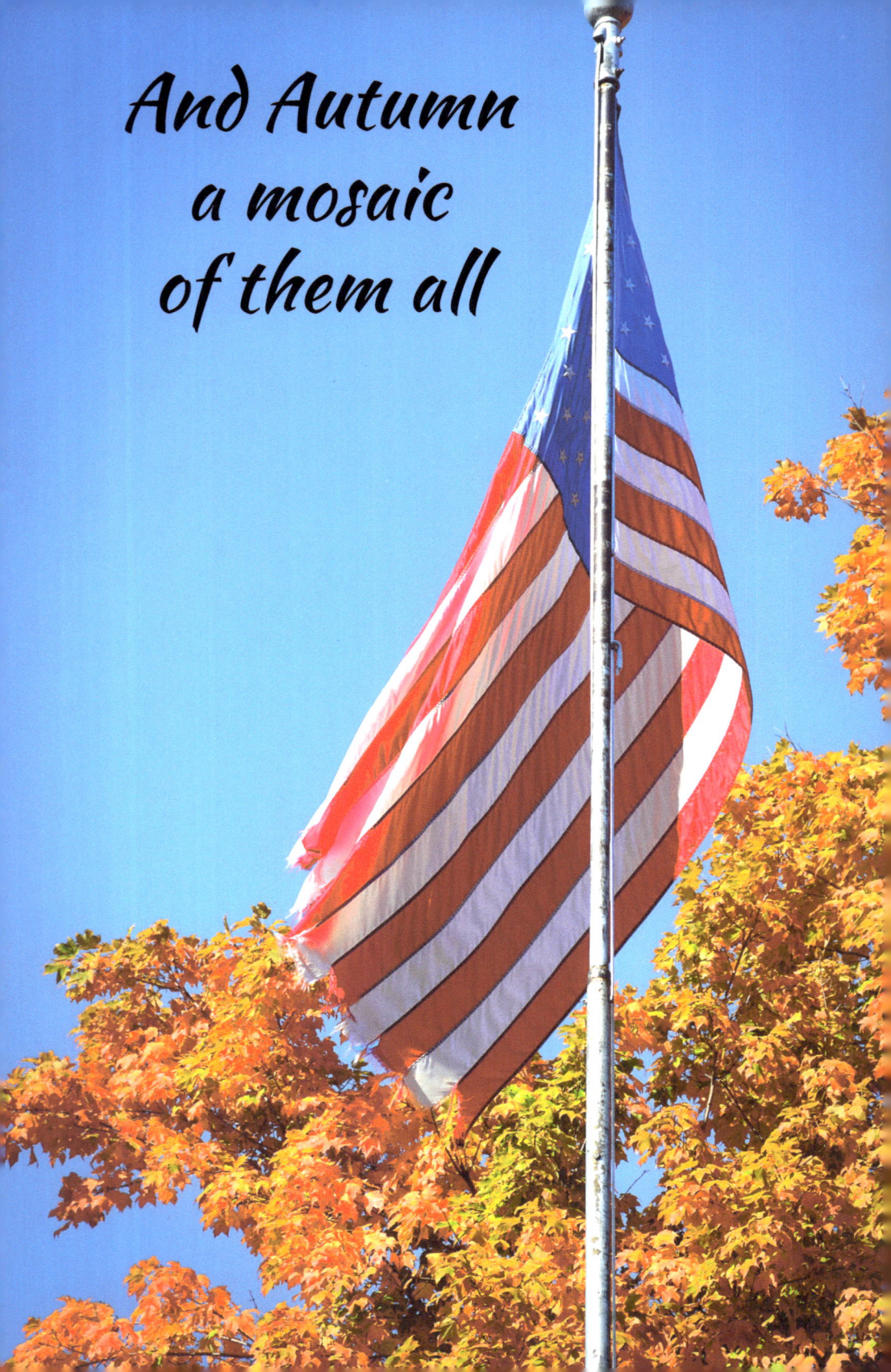

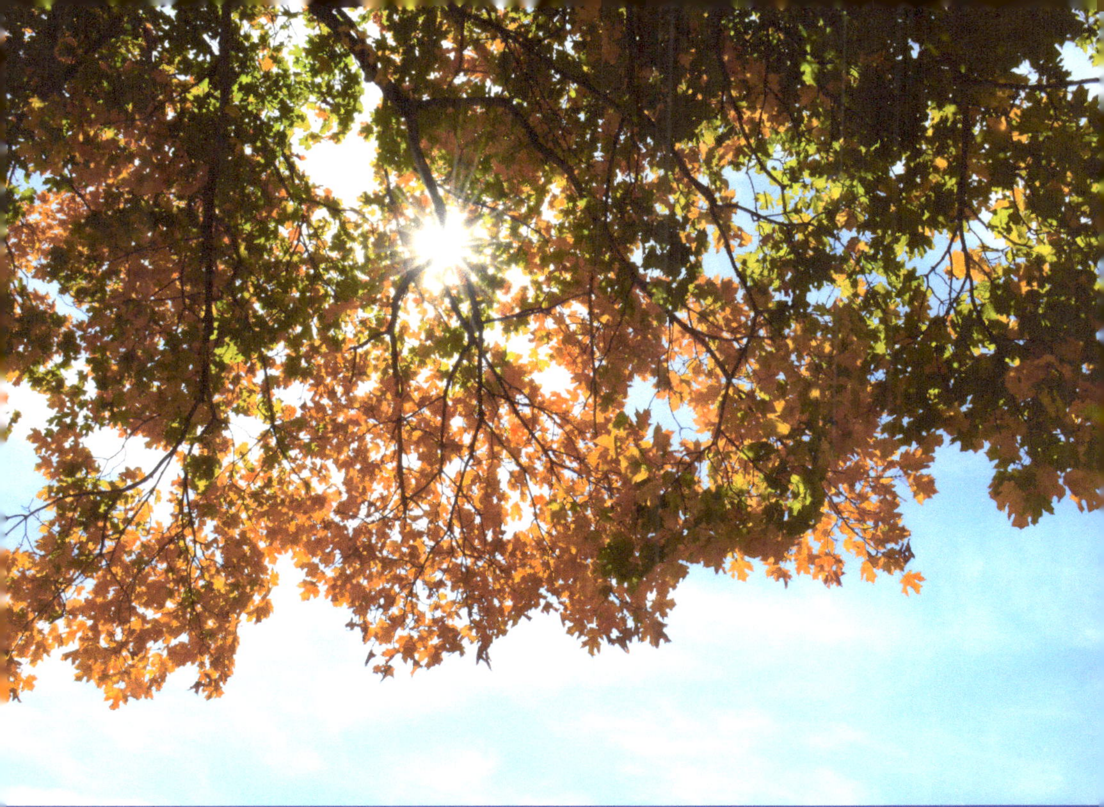

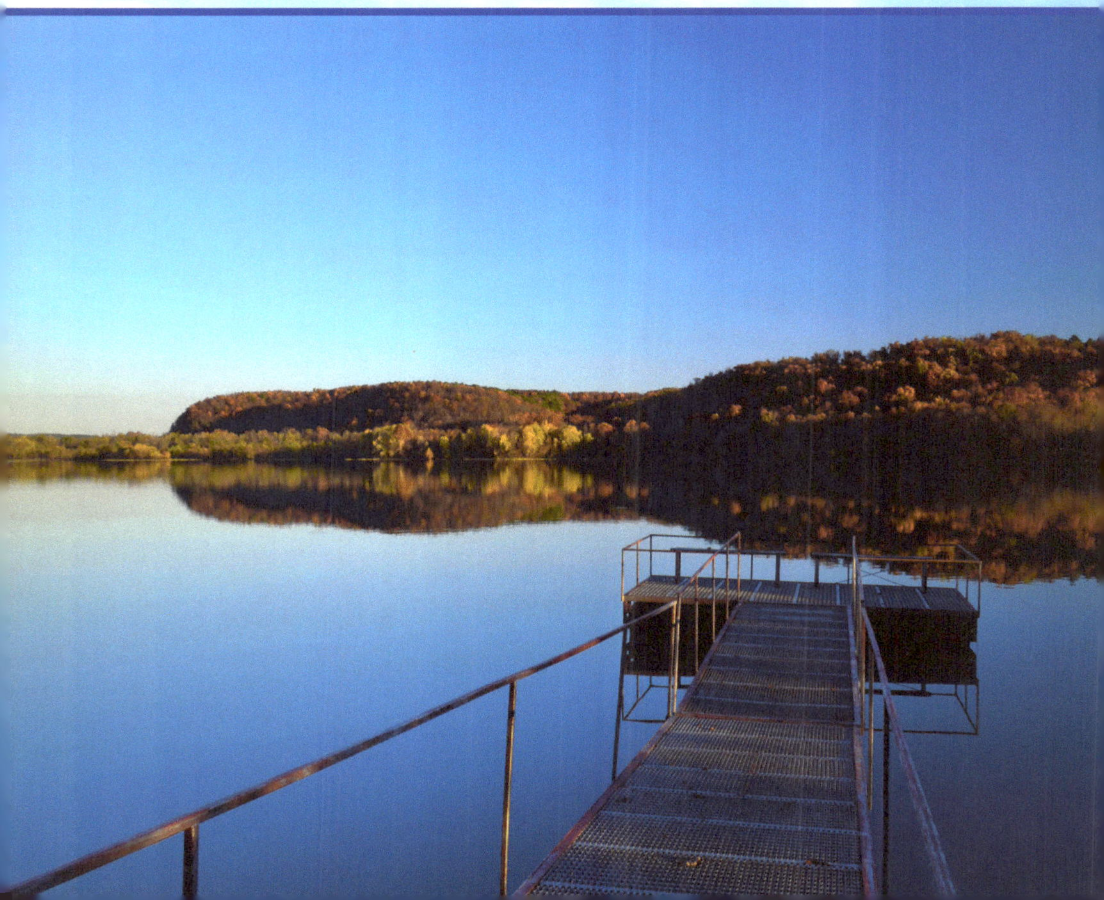

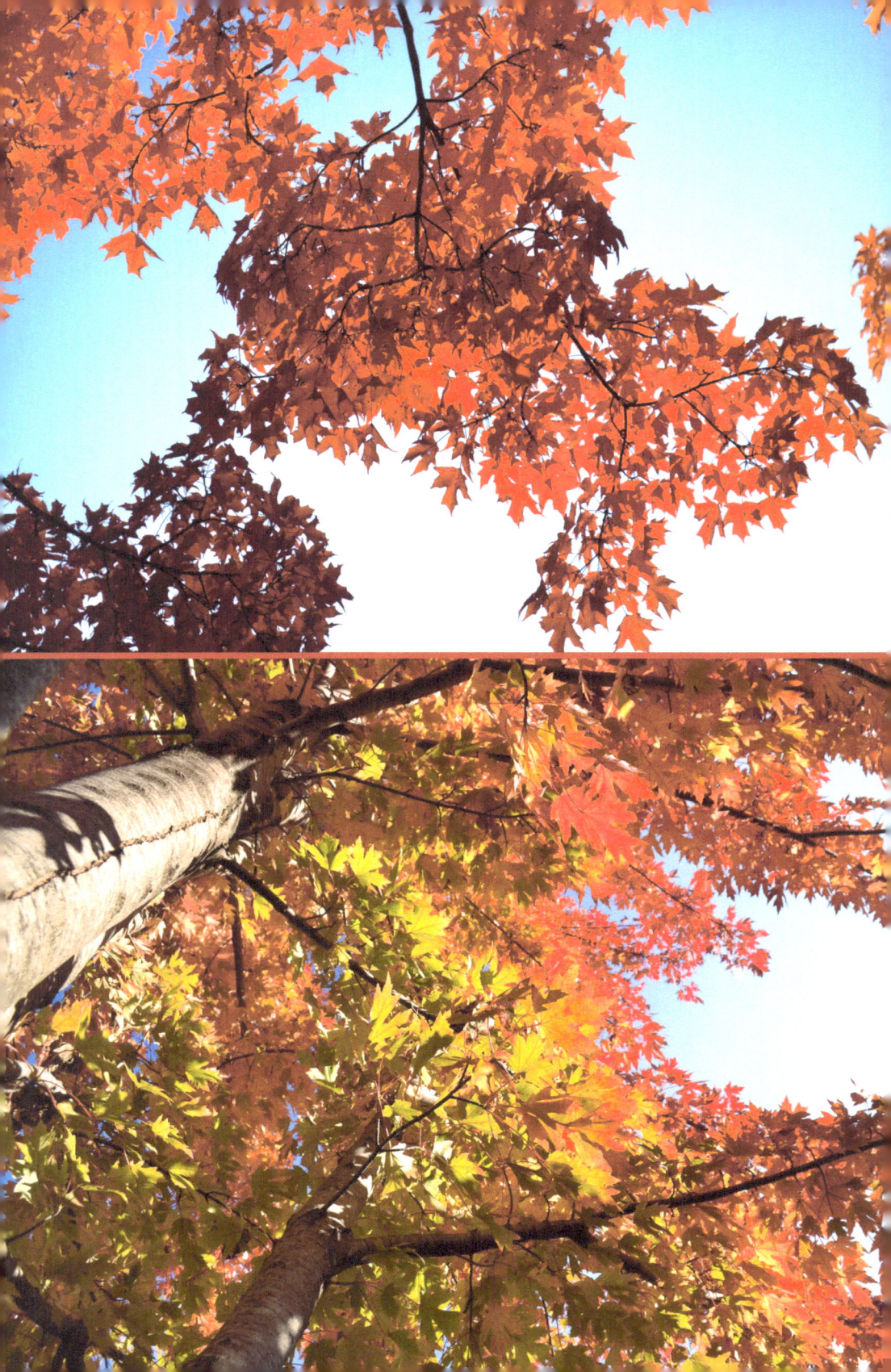

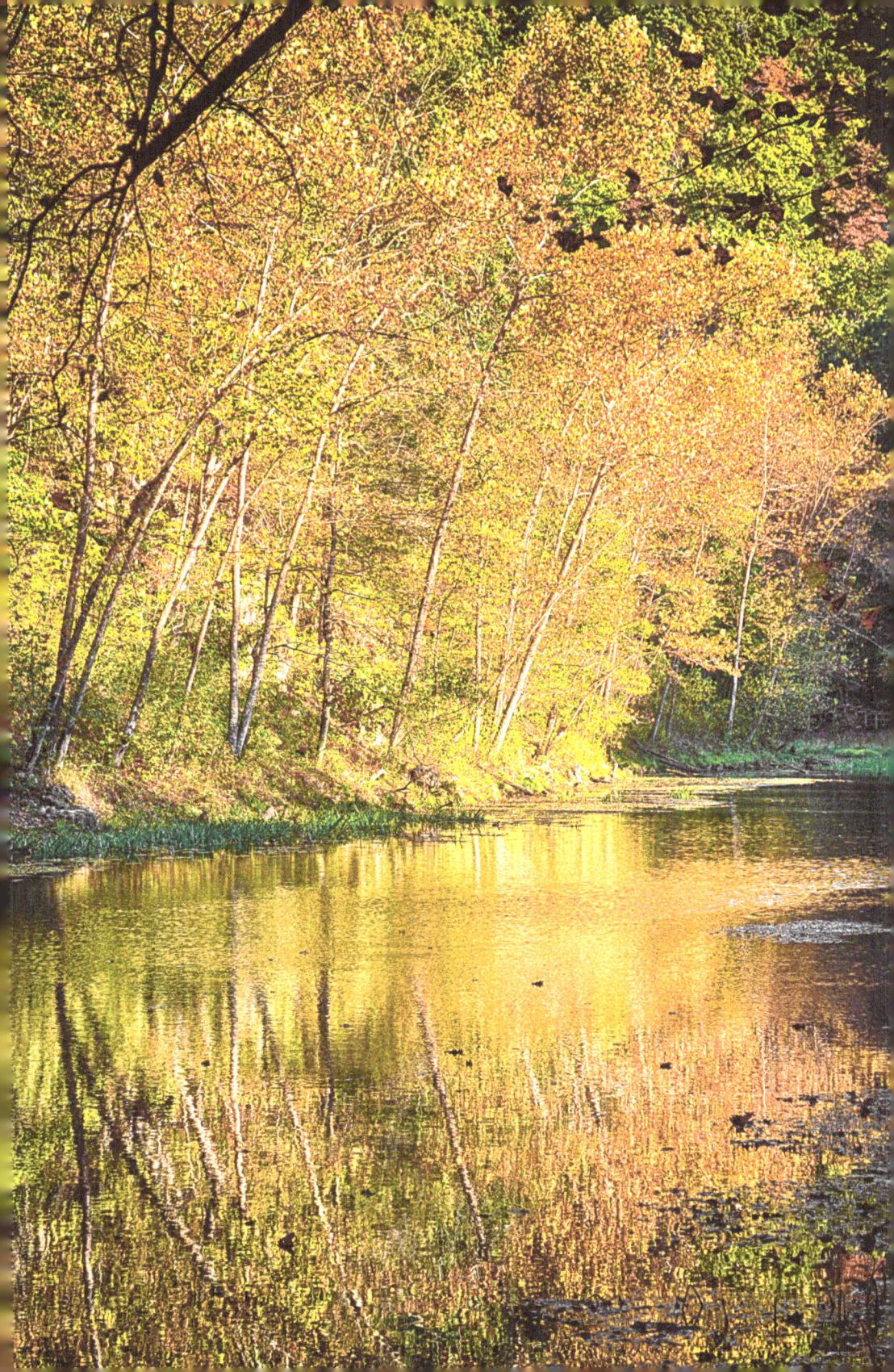

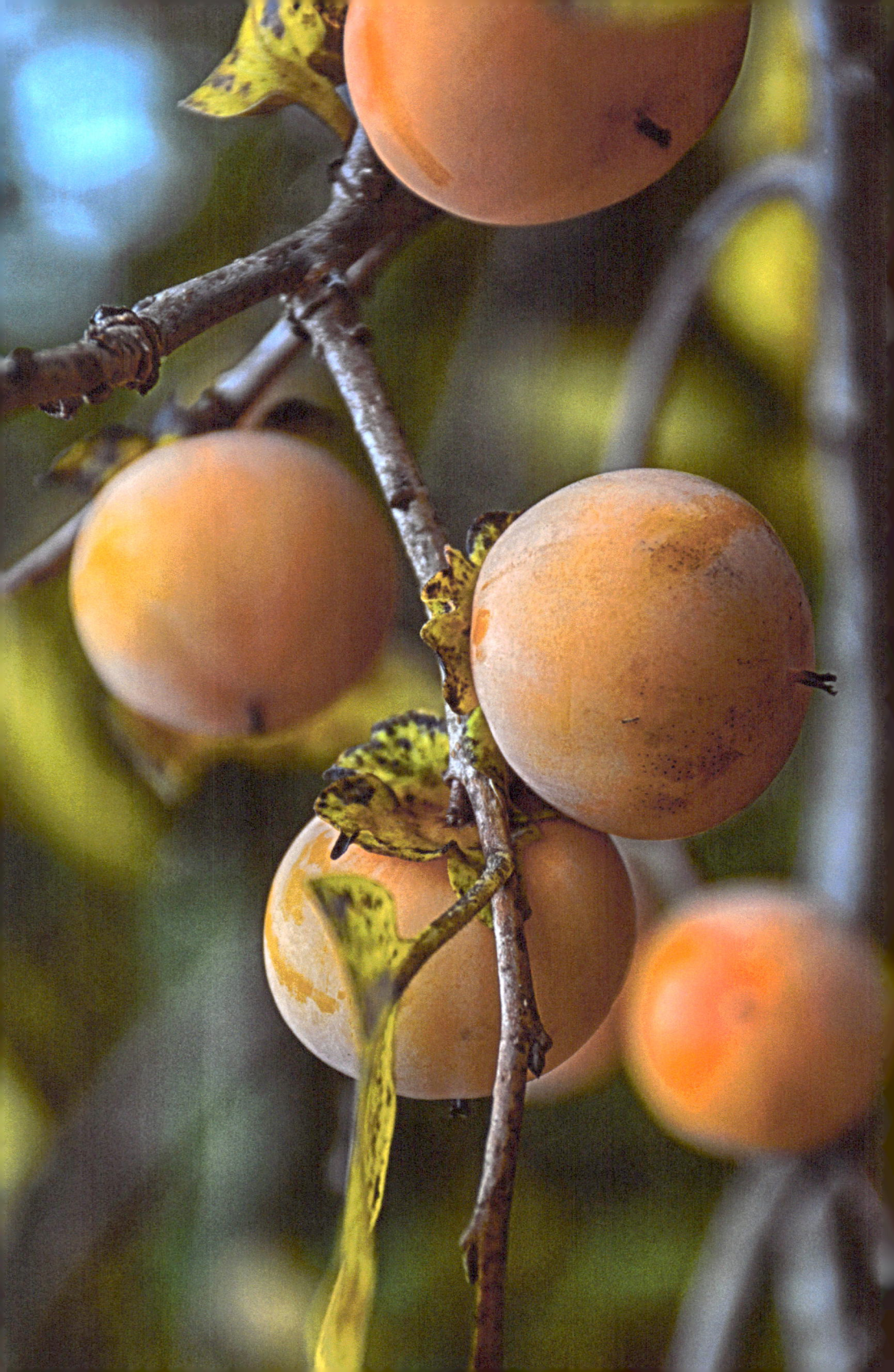

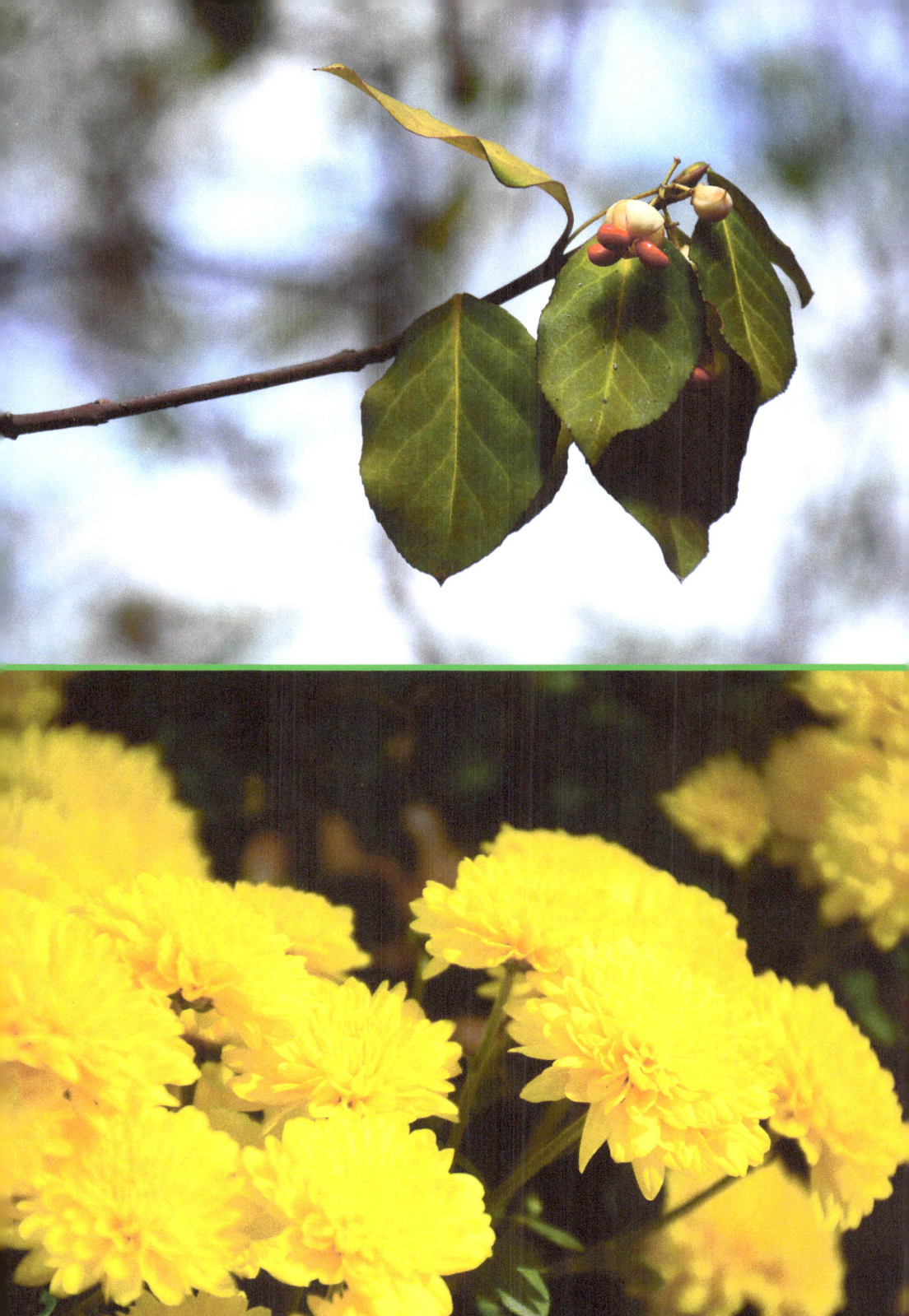

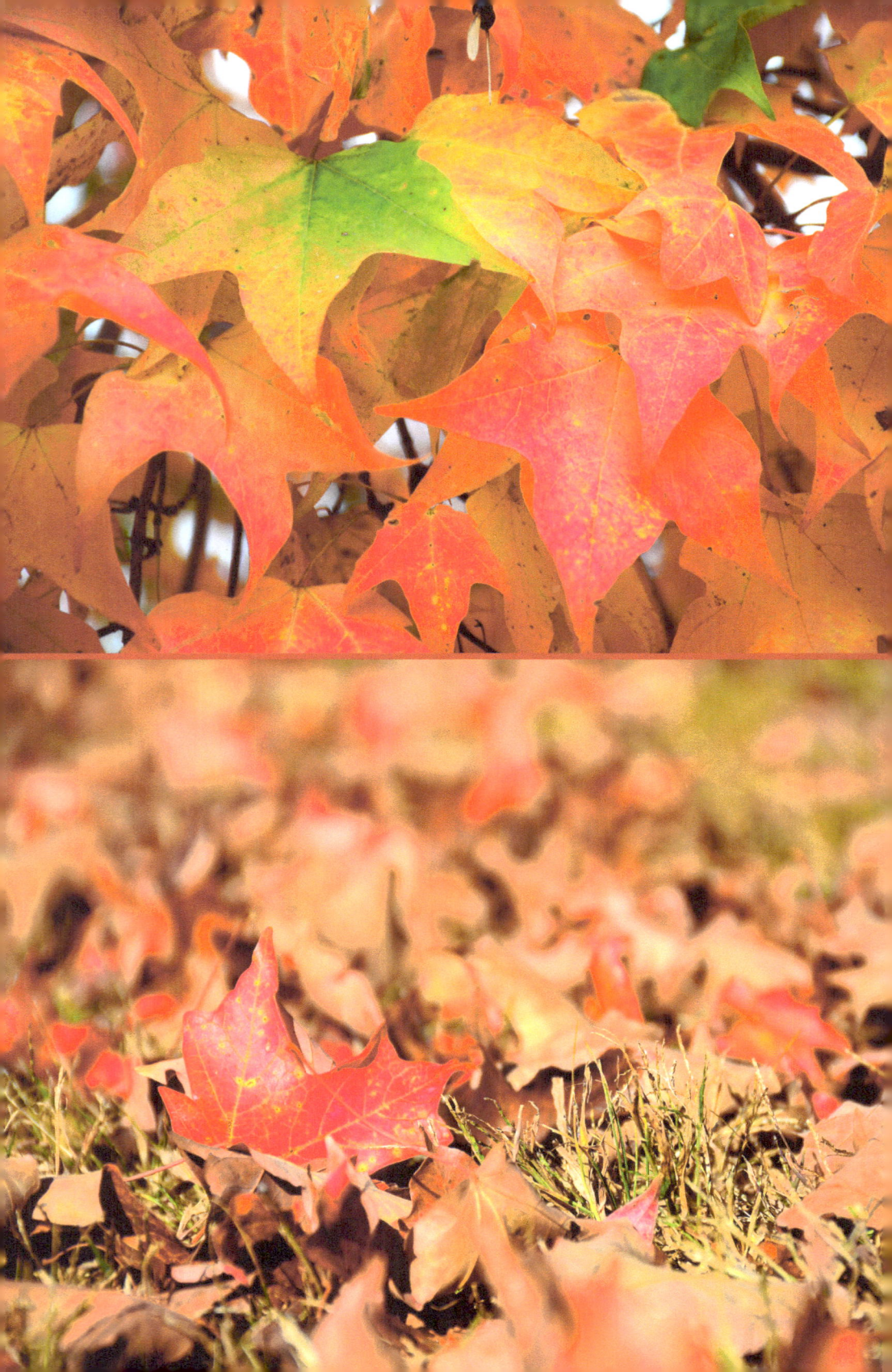

The Four Seasons through Photographs

All Images Copyrighted © 2018
Jane Ballard

Jane Ballard Photography
1100 N Prosperity Ave
Joplin MO 64801
417-501-9960
jane@janeballard.com
www.janeballard.com

Follow Jane Ballard Photography
on Facebook

@JBallardPhoto2
Twitter
Instagram
Pinterest

www.ingramcontent.com/pod-product-compliance
Lightning Source LLC
Chambersburg PA
CBHW040303220526
45473CB00002B/566